Ev

CW00364026

Welcome to Berlin!

This opening fold-out contains a general map of Berlin to help you visualise the 6 districts discussed in this guide, and 4 pages of valuable information, handy tips and useful addresses.

Discover Berlin through 6 districts and 6 maps

A Unter den Linden / Friedrichstadt / Museumsinsel

B Scheunenviertel / Prenzlauer Berg

C Alexanderplatz / Nikolaiviertel / Friedrichshain

D Kreuzberg

E Tiergarten / Potsdamer Platz / Schöneberg

F Kurfürstendamm / Charlottenburg

For each district there is a double-page of addresses (restaurants – listed in ascending order of price – cafés, bars, tearooms, music venues and shops), followed by a fold-out map for the relevant area with the essential places to see (indicated on the map by a star ★). These places are by no means all that Berlin has to offer, but to us they are unmissable. The grid-referencing system (**A** B2) makes it easy for you to pinpoint addresses quickly on the map.

Transportation and hotels in Berlin

The last fold-out consists of a transportation map and 4 pages of practical information that include a selection of hotels.

Thematic index

Lists all the street names, sites and addresses featured in this guide.

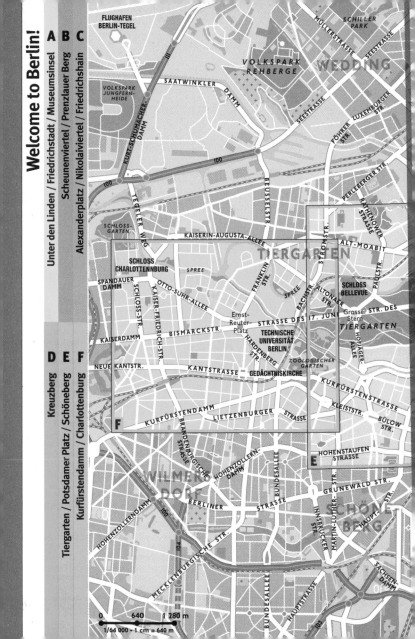

THE WALL

- Aug 12, 1961: the construction of the Wall begins. It will be 96 miles long, 12 feet high with 300 watchtowers.
- 1961–89: more than 239 people are killed trying to cross the Wall.
- Nov 9, 1989: fall of the Wall.

The remains of the Wall
Bernauer Strasse (**B** B2)
Fragment and monument.
Potsdamer Platz (**E** D4)
Fragment.
Brandenburger Tor (**A** A3)
Red markings (2 ½ miles) on the sidewalks as far as Checkpoint Charlie.
East Side Gallery (**C** D4)
650-foot-long fragment.

POTSDAM

arge cultural store, selling books, CDs, German and nternational videos (DVDs).
Shopping malls
Kaufhof (**C** A2)
➤ Alexanderplatz
Potsdamer Platz
Arkaden (**E** D4)
➤ Potsdamer Platz
Friedrichstadt
Passagen (**A** C4)
➤ Französischestr. 68
Europa Center (**F** F3)
➤ Breitscheidplatz
Flea markets
Tiergarten (**E** C3)
➤ Str. of the 17. Juni
at-Sun 11am–5pm
rt and flea market overing several miles.
m Zeughaus (**A** D2)
➤ Am Kupfegraben
at-Sun 11am–5pm
he most attractive of the lea markets, with books, ecords and Eastern uropean crafts.
Moritzplatz (**D** D2)
➤ Sat-Sun 8am–4pm
Mountains of bric-à-brac.

Arkonaplatz (**B** C2)
➤ Sun 10am–4pm
The trendiest.
Credit cards
Note that foreign cards (Visa, AmEx etc.) are often refused.

BERLIN ANOTHER WAY

Berlin by bus
Lines 100 and 200
➤ Between the Zoologischer Garden and Alexanderplatz, or between Prenzlauerberg and Potsdamer Platz. Every 10 mins (30 mins, 2.10 €)
A tour of Berlin's most important monuments.
Berlin by boat
Many companies provide boat trips through the center or along the Havel.
Tour of the center (**A** E3)
➤ Schlossbrücke Pier
Tel. 536 36 00 March-Oct: daily at 10am, 11.10am, 2pm, 3.10pm (3 ½ hrs, 16 €)
Museumsinsel, Tiergarten,

Kreuzberg on the Spree and Landwehrkanal.
Toward Potsdam
➤ Wannsee Pier
Tel. 536 36 00
Mid-April-end Sep: Tue-Sun 11am (6 hrs return, 13 €)
From Wannsee Lake to Werder Island, via the Pfaueninsel and Potsdam.

VIEWS OF THE CITY

Debis Haus (**E** D4)
The most modern: from the top of a building in Potsdamer Platz.
Siegessäule (**E** B3)
The highest: from below the golden wings of Goldelse.
Reichstag (**E** D2)
The most historical: from the dome, above the great hall of the reunified Bundestag.
Fernsehturm (**C** A2)
From the revolving restaurant, 680 feet above the city.

EXCURSIONS

Treptower Park
➔ S-Bahn Treptower Park
Large East Berlin park, with a monument to the Russian soldiers killed during World War Two.
Botanischer Garten
➔ S-Bahn Botanischer Garten Tel. 838 50 100
Daily 9am–dusk
A sumptuous 82-foot high glasshouse with 18,000 plant species.
Forst Grunewald
➔ S-Bahn Grunewald
Immense forest in the southwest of Berlin.
Wannsee
➔ S-Bahn Wannsee
The largest lake in the city: several miles of beach and the Pfaueninsel, with its peacocks and gardens.
Dahlem Museumszentrum
➔ Lansstr. 8,
Dahlem Dorf subway station Tel. 830 14 38 Tue-Fri 10am–6pm; Sat-Sun 11am–6pm
Ethnography and non-European arts.
Potsdam
Schloss Sanssouci
➔ Tel. (0331) 969 42 02
Daily 8.30am–5pm (9am–4pm Nov-March)
The rococo Versailles of Frederick the Great.
Dutch Quarter
➔ Friedrich-Eberstr., Kurfürstentr., Gutenbergstr.
Built in the 18th century, it houses art galleries, cafés and busy restaurants.
Filmstudio Babelsberg
➔ Grossbeerenstr.
Tel. (018 5) 721 27 17
March-Oct: daily 10am–6pm
One of the largest movie studios in Europe between 1917 and 1945.

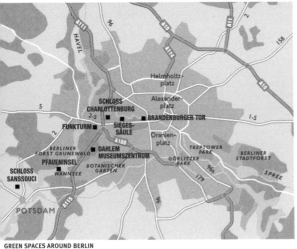

GREEN SPACES AROUND BERLIN

MARX AND ENGELS

HACKESCHE HÖFE

Biergarten
Gardens filled with large tables and wooden benches, and buzzing with life. Convivial atmosphere and typically German: perfect for a good beer and sausage!

Specialties
Curry Wurst: sausage with a curry and ketchup sauce.
Bulette: spiced, minced meat ball.
Eisbein auf Sauerkraut: ham on sauerkraut. (cabbage)
Berliner Weisse: blonde beer with raspberry syrup.

MUSEUMS

Information
Staatliche Museum zu Berlin
→ *Tel. 266 2987*
www.smb.spk-berlin.de
Information on the major museums.

3-Tage Karte
→ *On sale in all participating museums.*

Price 10€ (5€ concessions) Transferable ticket valid for three days for admission to over 60 museums, including the largest ones.

Guided tours
Bärentouren
→ *Tel. 46 60 44 97*
Themed tours.
Individuelle Touren
→ *Tel. 892 13 38*
Individual tours.
Zeitreisen Berlin
→ *Tel. 44 02 44 50*
Historical tours.

BARS AND CLUBS

There are many *Kneipen*, cocktail bars, *Biergarten*, clubs, cultural centers and nightclubs of all varieties. Anything goes in most clubs: the most far-out or trendiest clothes can be seen under the same roof as jeans and T-shirts. Entry fees are negotiable for groups. Admission to clubs is often free after 4am.

SHOWS

Listings
Tip and Zitty
→ *Bimonthly, available from newspaper vendors*
www.zitty.de
Berlin life: movies, clubs, theaters, concerts and useful addresses.
030
→ *Monthly and bimonthly; from bars, clubs and some theaters*
Small, free publications listing parties and concerts.

Reservations
→ *On websites such as* www.deutschland-tickets.de, *by phone, from the kiosks* (Theaterkasse), *or direct from the theaters*
Beware: the large venues are often booked out several months in advance (Deutsche Oper, Philharmonie, etc.).

On the day
Abendskasse
→ *In person one hour*

before the show
Box offices are reopened and a waiting list is operated. Unclaimed tickets are re-sold 30 minutes before the performance.
Hekticket (C A2)
→ *Karl-Liebknecht-Str. 12*
Tel. 24 31 24 31
www.hekticket.de
Last-minute tickets: concerts, theater, opera...

SHOPPING

Department stores
KaDeWe (F F4)
Germany's answer to Harrods: the store that stocks everything.
Galeries Lafayette (A C4)
→ *Französischestr. 23*
Tel. 20 94 80
Mon-Sat 10am–8pm
Predominantly luxury ready-to-wear, accessories and perfumery.
Dussmann (A C2)
→ *Friedrichstr. 90. Tel. 202 50*
Mon-Sat 10am–10pm

SCHINKELMUSEUM

MUSEUMSINSEL

PERGAMON MUSEUM

★ Brandenburger Tor (A A3)

→ Pariser Platz

Built in 1788 by Langhans after the model of the propylaea in Athens, the Brandenburg Gate had a Quadriga on its top, which Napoleon confiscated in 1806 and the Prussian army retrieved in 1814. A symbol of peace and then of German nationalism, the Gate ended up in East Germany when the Wall was built. Its reopening on December 22, 1989, made it an emblem of reunification.

★ Holocaust-Mahnmal (A A3)

www.holocaust-mahnmal.de

This project by the American architect Peter Eisenman opened in 2005 after years of deliberation. The 2,700 tombstones are made of shiny black stone and, somehow, the simplicity of the design makes the memorial even more moving. The information center that is yet to be built will focus on historical facts and list the names of the six million Jews assassinated in the death camps.

★ Unter den Linden (A D3)

Baroque ornamentation (Zeughaus), classical colonnades (Staatsoper, Humboldt Universität), neoclassical pillars (Kronprinzenpalais, Altes Palais) and a Doric portico (Neue Wache, Schinkel's masterpiece) form a guard of honor for the statue of Frederick the Great (1851).

★ Gendarmenmarkt (A C4)

→ Huguenot Museum in the Französischer Dom

Tel. 229 17 60 Tue-Sat noon–5pm; Sun 11am–5pm

Twin domes (Von Gonthard, 1785) crown the Deutscher and Französischer Dom (1701–5), built for the French and German Calvinists. Since the fall of the Wall, restaurants and cafés have opened onto this glorious paved square, where crowds sit in summer in the shade of the trees.

★ Bebelplatz (A D3)

St Hedwig's Cathedral (1747–

73) looks like an upturn cup, and the Baroque curves of the old library (1774–80) like a *Komm* Only the Staatsoper ref the initial plans for the Forum devised by Frederick II (1740–86). evening, a white light g through a glass paving stone at the center of the square. Below, the emp shelves of a library reca great Nazi *auto de fe* of 10, 1933, when 20,000 'anti-German' books we up in smoke below the university's windows.

★ Schinkelmuseum (A

→ Friedrichswerdersche Kirche, Werderstr.

Tue-Sun 10am–6pm

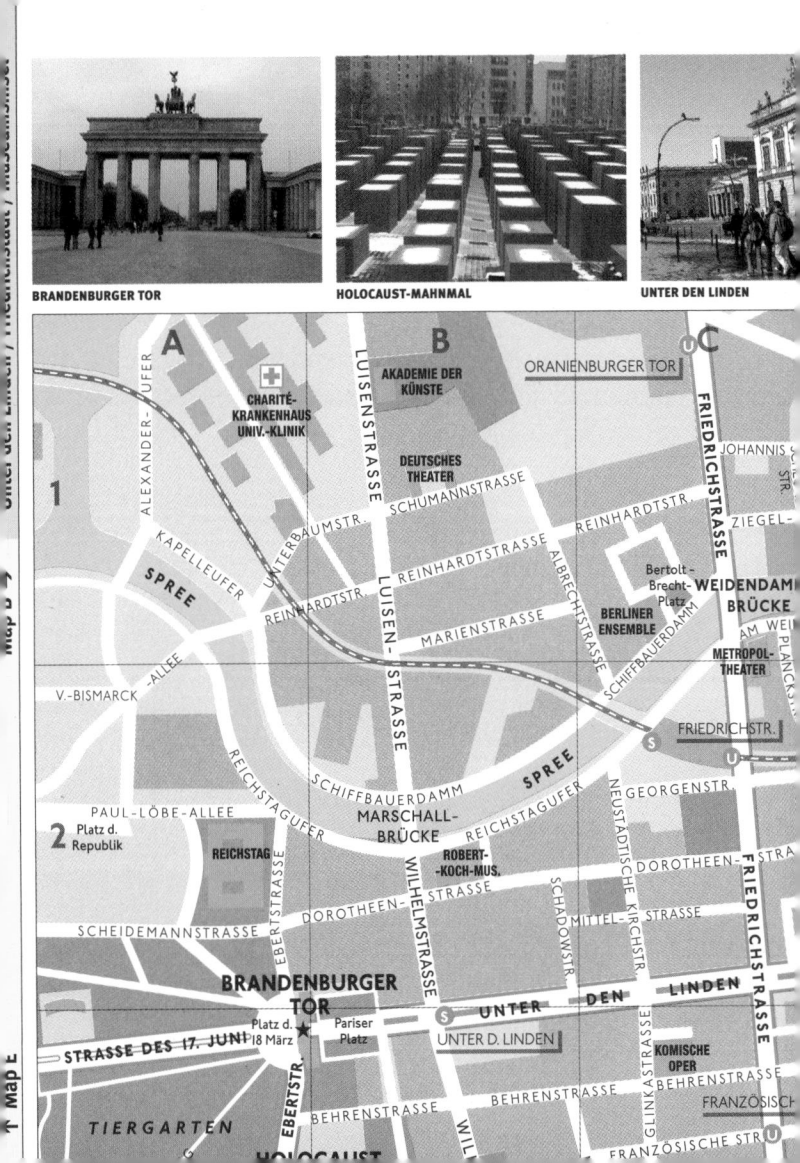

BRANDENBURGER TOR

HOLOCAUST-MAHNMAL

UNTER DEN LINDEN

Unter den Linden, in the heart of historical Berlin (Mitte), is being gradually restored to its former splendor. Setting off from the Brandenburg Gate, visitors can take a trip back through two centuries of German monumentalism, from the former Soviet embassy and the contemporary buildings on Friedrichstrasse, to Frederick II's Bebelplatz. Modern, classical or Baroque, the majestic façades convey the austere grandeur of the Prussians. At the end of the avenue, opposite the site of the former royal palace, stands the Museumsinsel, the cultural Acropolis of the city popularly known as Athens-on-the-Spree.

OXYMORON

LUTTER & WEGNER

IMBISS, RESTAURANTS

Suppenbörse (A D2)
→ Dorotheenstr. 43
Tel. 20 45 59 03 Mon-Fri
11am–8pm; Sat 11.30–6pm
(closed Sat in summer)
Recipes from India, France, Swabia or Hungary. Every week you choose from six new and filling soups. Take out or eat in. Dishes 3–5 €.

Ständige Vertretung (A B2)
→ Schiffbauerdamm 8
Tel. 28 59 87 36
Daily 10am–1am
The photos of *Wessis* ('from the west') politicians on the walls leave no room for doubt: the sympathies of the owner, from Bonn, lie with West Germany. Berlin *Buletten*, of course, but also specialties from the Rhineland. Dishes 8–13 €.

Samâdhi (A B3)
→ Wilhelmstr. 77
Tel. 22 48 88 50
Tue-Sat noon–3pm, 6–11pm;
Sun noon–3pm
What this place lacks in decor, it makes up for in the quality of its food. Oriental vegetarian cuisine, subtle flavors and very good value. One of the few restaurants in this area, where embassies are ubiquitous. Do try the

ginger and lemon flavored dishes. Menus 9–12 €.

Oxymoron (A E1)
→ Rosenthalerstr. 40/41
Tel. 28 39 18 86
Daily 11am–midnight
At the heart of Hackesche Höfe, a former garage has given way to a theatrical decor. Carpets from the 1950s, velvet sofas and sparkling chandeliers: a haven of tranquility much appreciated by Berliners. Good cuisine, too. Dishes 9–17 €.

Lutter & Wegner (A D3)
→ Charlottenstr. 56
Tel. 20 29 540 Daily 11am–2am; service noon–midnight
The best of Austrian and German cooking, with a view of the Gendarmenmarkt from this old-fashioned Berlin brasserie filled with contemporary artworks. Dishes 17–25 €.

Französischer Hof (A D3)
→ Jägerstr. 56
Tel. 20 17 71 70
Daily 11am–midnight
This large brasserie is popular with chic Berliners, who monopolize the terrace in the summer to enjoy the concerts given in front of the Konzerthaus. Inside, wonderful Jugendstil decor, stylish global cuisine and a flurry of waiters swirling around in a perfect choreography.

HIKISCHE TEESTUBE

BERLINER ENSEMBLE

FRIEDRICHSTADT PASSAGEN

In the evenings, jazz or *Kabarett* in the piano-bar. Dishes 15-19€; menu 25€.

TEAROOMS

Opernpalais (A D3)
→ *Unter den Linden 5*
Tel. 20 26 83 Daily 8am–8pm
Smart elderly ladies, trendy young Berliners, and women in evening dresses gather beneath the moldings and gilt work of the Prinzessinnen Palace. The terrace is popular for afternoon tea or a drink before the opera.

Tadshikische Teestube (A D2)
→ *Am Festungsgraben 1*
Tel. 204 11 12
Mon-Fri 5pm–midnight;
Sat-Sun 3pm–midnight
A journey to Tadjikistan awaits he who enters this house: a veritable artisanal gem filled with wooden sculptures and paintings. Come and take off your shoes before relaxing on the rugs and cushions. Reserve to avoid disappointment!

CLASSICAL MUSIC, THEATERS

Staatsoper (A D3)
→ *Unter den Linden 7*
Tel. 20 35 45 55
Ticket office: Mon-Fri 11am–
7pm; Sat-Sun & public hols 2–7pm and one hour before performance
www.staatsoper/berlin.org
The oldest opera house in the world, commissioned by Frederick II, was built in 1743 as a classical temple of music. Wonderful recitals and operas are staged here.

Komische Oper (A C3)
→ *Behrenstr. 55-57*
Tel. 20 26 06 66
Ticket office: Mon-Sat 11am–7pm; Sun & public hols 1pm–one hour before performance
www.komische-oper-berlin.com
This is an opera house for everyone: great classics of comic opera and works performed in German.

Konzerthaus (A C4)
→ *Gendarmenmarkt 2*
Tel. 20 30 92 101
Ticket office: Mon-Sat noon–7pm; Sun noon–4pm.
www.konzerthaus.de
Hung with chandeliers, Schinkel's auditorium has superb acoustics for the Rundfunk-Symfonie-Orchester and Rundfunk-chor. Exceptional organs at the rear of the stage.

Berliner Ensemble (A B1)
→ *Bertolt-Brecht-Platz 1*
Tel. 28 40 81 55
Ticket office: Mon-Fri 8am–6pm; Sat-Sun 11am–6pm
www.berliner-ensemble.de
The theater of Bertolt Brecht, then of Heiner Müller, is now run by Claus Peymann. Works by the great masters as well as by contemporary writers.

Deutsches Theater (A A1)
→ *Schumannstr. 13a*
Tel. 28 44 12 25
Ticket office: Mon-Sat 11am–6.30pm; Sun 3–6.30pm
Berlin's oldest theater, made famous by Max Reinhardt when he ran it in the 1920s. Today, Thomas Langhof mounts revivals of great classics.

BAR, CLUB

Cinéma Café (A E1)
→ *Rosenthalerstr. 39*
Tel. 28 06 415
Daily noon–3pm
A very long, narrow café bustling with people day and night. Find a spot in which to drink your beer: at the piano, next to the window or at a table on the sidewalk. Terrace in the courtyard in summer.

Kalkscheune (A C1)
→ *Johannisstr. 2*
Tel. 59 00 43 40
www.kalkscheune.de
A vast complex of rooms for diverse events: rock or jazz concerts, cabaret evenings, dance or disco.

SHOPPING

Berlin Story (A B3)
→ *Unter den Linden 10*
Tel. 20 45 38 42
Daily 10am–7pm
Everything to do with Berlin, from keyrings to specialist books. At the rear are two models of the classical city and the royal palace, now gone.

Friedrichstadt Passagen (A C3)
→ *Friedrichstr. 68 Mon-Sat 10am–8pm (6pm Sat)*
A sumptuous and labyrinthine shopping mall, whose stores underground are connected by passageways.

Weinhandel Lutter & Wegner (A C3)
→ *Charlottenstr. 56*
Tel. 20 29 540
Daily noon–midnight
A grand store offering a guided tour of the tastes of the German charcuterie: cured meats, sausages and black pudding washed down with a glass of wine, to enjoy here or to take out.

Grüne Erde (A D1)
→ *Oranienburgerstr. 1-3*
Tel. 20 45 59 03 Mon-Fri 11am–8pm; Sat 10am–6pm
A temple dedicated to well-being! Everything sold here is made of 100% natural ingredients for you and your home.

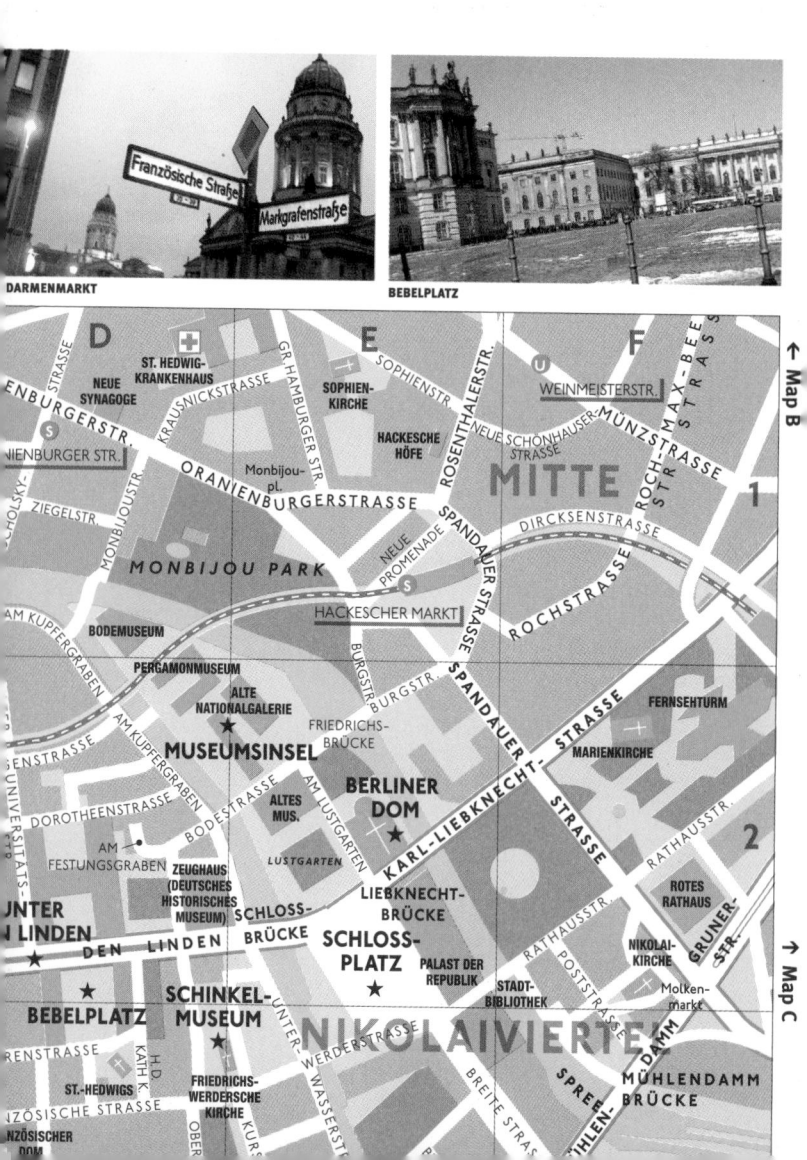

DARMENMARKT

BEBELPLATZ

← Map B

↑ Map C

Map (street names):
WISSENSCH. · MOHRENSTR · NIEDERWALLSTRASSE · GERTRAUDENSTRASSE · SPREE · KAN · NEUE · ROSSSTRASSE · MER · KRAFENSTR. · KRONENSTR · GERTRAUDEN-BRÜCKE · WALLSTRASSE · TR. · Spittel-markt · SPITTELMARKT · ALTE JAKOBSTR. · LEIPZIGER STRASSE · SEYDELSTR. · NEUE GRÜNSTRASSE · ALTE JAKOBSTR. · KRAUSENSTRASSE · BEUTHSTR. · SEBASTIANSTRASSE · STRASSE · JERU- SALEMER STR. · ZENSTRASSE · KOMMANDANTENSTRASSE · STRASSE · SCHUT- · AXEL-SPRINGER STRASSE · MARKGRAFENSTR. · ZIMMERSTRASSE · KOCHSTRASSE · D · E · F · 4

0 100 200 m

MUSEUM

BERLINER DOM AND SCHLOSSPLATZ

...ster of 19th-century Classicism in Berlin, Friedrich Schinkel (1–1841) was also the er of architectural cticism, evident in the Gothic brick church (4–30) that houses his eum. The gallery is d with sketches, uscripts and technical ctions. The nave boasts e neoclassical statues.

Museumsinsel (A D2) el. 28 39 74 44 Tue–Sun 1–6pm (10pm Thu) /.museumsinsel-berlin.de mazing complex of eums built like many ples to the grandeur of ssia (1830–1930). The amon, Altes Museum

and Alte Nationalgalerie are now home to the reunified collections. The reopening of the Bode Museum in 2006 marked the end of the ambitious renovation program started in 1989.

Alte Nationalgalerie
The best-known German and European 19th-century artists are represented here: Von Menzel, Caspar D. Friedrich, Manet, etc.

Pergamon Museum
Separating the two sides of this vast museum stands the enormous Pergamon altar. To the left, Hellenistic and Latin statues and mosaics. To the right, the market gate from Miletus (120 BC) faces the blue and

gold archway of the Ishtar Gate, which marks the entrance to the department of Near-Eastern Antiquities and Islamic Art.

Altes Museum
Resembling a Greek temple, Schinkel's impressive building houses one of the finest ancient collections in the world: statues from Ancient Greece to the late Roman era, vases, jewelry and gold and silver crockery.

★ Berliner Dom (A E2)
→ Lustgarten. Tel. 202 690 Mon–Sat 9am–8pm; Sun noon–8pm
Beneath the opulent nave of the Protestant cathedral, rebuilt in 1905 in a rather overpowering neo-Baroque

style, are 90 Hohenzollern tombs (ceremonial coffins of Frederick I and Sophie-Charlotte in the style of Schlüter, and that of the Great Elector).

★ Schlossplatz (A E3)
All that remains of the royal palace, bombed then blown up in 1950, is the balcony from which Karl Liebknecht proclaimed the Spartacist republic on Nov 9, 1918. The Palast der Republik, former East Germany's parliament and people's leisure center, has stood on the site since 1976. Although saved from demolition by the mobilisation of certain Ossis, its future residence is still uncertain.

MUSEUM FÜR NATURKUNDE

GEDENKSTÄTTE BERLINER MAUER

★ **Hackesche Höfe** (B C4)
→ *Rosenthalerstr. 41 / Sophienstr. 6*
The façades designed in 1906 by Kurt Berndt and August Endell, whose style was similar to that of the Viennese Sezession, transformed this labyrinth of inner courtyards into a masterpiece of Jugendstil: ceramic tiles, vibrant colors and an interplay of curves and geometric figures. Completely restored, they now house popular cafés, a movie theater, a theater, galleries and showrooms.

★ **Sophienstrasse** (B C4)
A traditional narrow street typical of living conditions in the 18th and 19th centuries: behind the stuccoed façades is a sequence of brick courtyards. At no. 18 you will see the neo-Renaissance earthenware portico of the Artisans' House, a key site in Communist history. Nearby stands the Baroque church tower of the Sophienkirche (1712–34).

★ **Neue Synagoge** (B C4)
→ *Oranienburgerstr. 28-30*
Tel. 88 02 83 00
May-Aug: Sun-Mon 10am–8pm; Tue-Fri 10am–6pm (5pm Fri); Sep-April: Sun-Fri 10am–6pm (2pm Fri);
This Byzantine dome sparkling in the sunshine belongs to the great synagogue (1866), torched during Kristallnacht, then bombed. Behind the Moorish arches of the façade, rebuilt in 1995, a museum examines the role of the Jewish community in Berlin.

★ **Tacheles** (B B4)
→ *Oranienburgerstr. 54/56*
Tel. 282 61 85
This artistic squat, a symbol of alternative culture, has managed to survive the property developers and tourist coaches since 1990, and finally the council has agreed to help the area retain its artistic ambience. Studios, a movie theater and an auditorium have been built in the immense building covered with frescos and graffiti. To the right of the entrance, the steel dragon of the Zapata Café belches fire over customers' heads.

★ **Brechthaus** (B A3)
→ *Chausseestr. 125*
Tel. 283 05 70 44 Guided every 30 mins Tue-Thu 10–11.30am; Thu 5–6.30pm; Fri 10–11.30am; Sat 9.30am–1.30pm; Sun 11am–6pm (every hour) Restaurant: Tue-Sat 6–9pm; www.lfbrecht.de
This was the home of Bertolt Brecht and Helene Weigel from 1953 to 1956. In the basement, the Kel

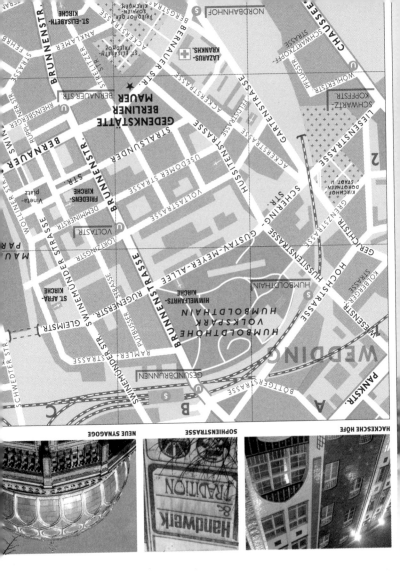

NEUE SYNAGOGE

SOPHIENSTRASSE

HACKESCHE HÖFE

North of Mitte, the Scheunenviertel ('barn district'), with its galleries, lofts and bars, has become a trendy bohemian area since reunification. It is hard to believe that before World War Two these restored stucco façades concealed squalid *Mietskasernen*, home to the communities which were then regarded as 'lower classes': the laborers, crooks and the Jewish community. Further out, in Prenzlauer Berg, renovated buildings stand next to peeling walls, which are gradually disappearing, while bars and alternative arts centers are opening their doors to young people in search of cheap and trendy ways to relax in the evenings.

ZOSCH

SCHWARZE PUMPE

IMBISS, RESTAURANTS

Konnopke (B E2)
→ *Schönhauser Allee 44a*
Mon-Fri 6am–8pm
The oldest *Curry Wurst* in the city, run by the same family since the 1930s. Dishes 1.25–3.50 €.

Naan (B D2)
→ *Oderberger Str. 49*
Tel. 44 05 84 14
Daily noon–midnight
Simple, tasty, home-cooked cuisine from southern India, best enjoyed with a *kashmiri* or *yogi* tea, or an Indian lager. Dishes 3.10–5 €.

The Chop Bar (B E1)
→ *Pappelallee 29*
Tel. 44 03 62 76 Daily
4–11pm (midnight Sat-Sun)
A rather trendy Senegalese restaurant. On the walls are interesting African masks and paintings by youngs artist. World music in the background. Fried sweet potatoes and black beans. Dishes 3.50–5 €.

Gorki Park (B D3)
→ *Weinbergsweg 25*
Tel. 448 72 86
Daily 9.30am–2am
Hip retro feel with a 1950s interior. Enjoy Russian specialties such as salad laced with vodka dressing late into the night.

Dishes 3.50–12 €.

Zosch (B B4)
→ *Tucholskystr. 30*
Tel. 280 76 64
Daily 4pm–2am
A Mitte classic: generous omelets for intimate evenings for two or live ska music in the basement. Dishes 5–14 €

Walden (B D2)
→ *Chorinerstr. 35*
Tel. 44 900 25 Winter: daily
from 5pm (10am Sun);
Summer: Mon-Sat from 2pm
A candlelit restaurant with homemade food – even down to the bread and the pasta. Don't miss out on the potato cakes with fresh pan-fried salmon and spicy avocado mousse. Dishes 6.50–17 €.

BARS, CONCERTS

Beth Café (B B4)
→ *Tucholskystr. 40*
Tel. 281 31 35 Sun-Thu
noon–8pm; Fri 10am–3pm
Kosher food, right beside the synagogue.

Nemo (B D2)
→ *Oderberger Str. 46*
Mon-Sat 6pm–3am;
Sun 11am–3am
Surrounded by a growing retinue of trendy bars, the Kapitän Nemo has held the helm since the Wall came down. Lively conversation, chinking

BÜHNE **ACUD** **KAUF DICH GLÜCKLICH**

glasses and laughter: a sociable melee that the comic-strip paintings, eccentric decor and confusion of irregularly shaped tables fortunately do nothing to subdue.

Schwarze Pumpe (B D3)
→ Chorinerstr. 76
Tel. 449 69 39
Daily 9am–1am
At the heart of the LSD Viertel, this *Kneipe* owes its name to the petrol pump that is the central feature of the room. Big wooden tables at which students come to have breakfast or sit and read.

Wohnzimmer (B E1)
→ Lettestr. 6
Tel. 445 54 58
Daily 10am–4am
This 'living room' has been in the wars: broken-down couches and armchairs, dilapidated walls and lighting suitable for a blackout. People have been partying here every night for almost six years. Drink your beer at the bar (when there is space). If you want to chill out on the sofas, you need to get here in the afternoon.

Schlot Kunstfabrik (B B3)
→ Schlegelstr. 29
Tel. 448 21 60
Daily from 7.30pm.
Concerts from 8pm

A café offering musical entertainment in the basement of a former factory: soft lighting and no more than 20 tables. Modern jazz (Fri-Mon), *Kabarett* (Tue-Thu).

Volksbühne (B D4)
→ Rosa-Luxemburg-Platz
Tel. 247 67 72 *Opening times vary according to venue.*
www.volksbuehne-berlin.de
This former People's Theater is still avant-garde and politically engaged. The two auditoriums are certainly eclectic in their programming: salsa, tango and ballroom dancing (Grüner Salon, Wed-Fri 9pm); readings and songs (Roter Salon). At the weekend both become clubs, sometimes taking over the entire theater.

Acud (B C3)
→ Veteranenstr. 21
Tel. 44 35 94 99
www.acud.de
Club: Thu-Sat from 10pm
Threatened with closure, this cultural center has been saved by the locals. Behind the façade now undergoing renovation, there is art and music on every floor: reggae, bossa or hip-hop concerts in the café, theater, gallery, art movies and a club. Ideal for getting to know the more alternative residents

of the district.

Prater (B D2)
→ Kastanienallee 7-9
Tel. 448 56 88
Open daily from 4pm.
Club: Wed-Sat from 9pm.
Restaurant: Mon-Sat 6–11pm; Sun 10am–11pm
Pleasant *Biergarten* under the plane trees of a peaceful courtyard; but Prater is also an annex of the Volksbühne, a club playing house music, and a *Gaststätte* (restaurant) serving slightly pricey but very good German cuisine (à la carte 23 €; brunch on Sunday).

Kulturbrauerei (B E2)
→ Knaackstr. 97
Tel. 48 49 44 44
Behind the brick walls of a lavishly restored industrial brewery is an upmarket, trendy complex: theaters, *Kneipen*, galleries, two clubs (packed on Sat) and a multiplex movie theater.

SHOPPING

Weinerei (B C3)
→ Veteranenstr. 14
Tel. 440 69 83
Mon-Tue 3–8pm; Wed-Fri 1–8pm; Sat 11am–8pm
1,001 wines explained by an experienced sommelier who entrances the locals when he does wine tasting evenings. Let yourself be

tempted!

Frau Tulpe (B C3)
→ Veteranenstr. 19
Tel. 44 32 78 65 Mon-Fri 10am–8pm; Sat 11am–3pm
Tables for cutting fabric to order and rolls of fabric to choose from: welcome to the studio of Frau Tulpe, who creates 1970s-style bags and kitsch accessories.

Kauf Dich glücklich (B D2)
→ Oderbergerstr. 44
Tel. 44 35 21 82
Daily 1pm–8pm
On the large sidewalk of this street formerly divided by the Wall is the sprawl of a bazaar selling bric-à-brac and clothes. Trendy and not always particularly good value, but bargain hunters still flock here.

Tribaltools.de (B E2)
→ Lychener Str. 10
Tel. 35 10 21 03 Mon-Fri noon–8pm (4pm Sat)
www.tribaltools.de
The hub of Berlin's trance scene: records, CDs, bags, tribal T-shirts and DJs mixing music.

Jenny Paris (B B4)
→ Linienstr. 141
Tel. 27 59 40 34
Mon-Fri 2–7pm; Sat 2–4pm
In this tiny boutique, you will find a talented jewelry designer whose specialty is hair clips made of silver.

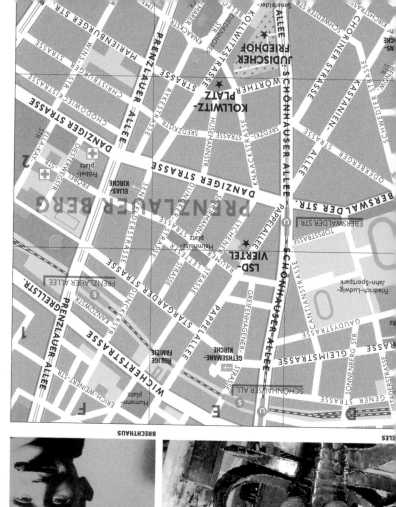

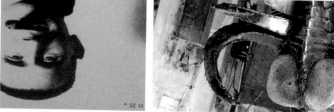

BRECHTHAUS

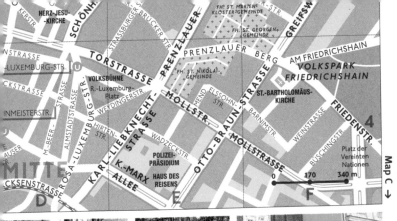

...HER FRIEDHOF

KOLLWITZPLATZ

LSD VIERTEL

Map C →

...rant serves Viennese
...es once cooked
...e. The house is next to
...orotheenstädtischer
...iof, where Brecht and
...l, Hegel, Schinkel,
...and Heinrich Mann
...uried.

useum für
rkunde (B A3)
*alidenstr. 43
...93 85 91 Sat-Sun
...–6pm; Tue-Fri 9.30am–*
*The museum is open but
...lls are under restoration.
...museum.hu-berlin.de*
...ren visiting the old
...al History Museum
...) are fascinated by
...npressive dinosaur
...tons: the 72-foot-long

brachiosaurus is the largest
skeleton of a reptile in the
world.

★ Jüdischer
Friedhof (B E3)
→ *Schönhauser Allee
Mon-Thu 8am-4pm (1pm Fri)*
Under a tall archway of
trees, ivy-covered tombs
lie beneath dead leaves.
The weather is gradually
eroding the names of Max
Liebermann and Meyerbeer,
as well as the scars inflicted
by the Nazis. The synagogue
at 53 Rykerstr. was spared
the flames on Kristallnacht
(Nov 9, 1938).

★ Gedenkstätte
Berliner Mauer (B B2)
→ *Dokumentationszentrum:*

*Bernauer Str. 111. Tel. 464 10 30
Wed-Sun 10am-5pm*
An immaculate section of
the Wall stands between
two huge sheets of metal,
seemingly frozen forever in
time. The information center
opposite charts the history
of the 'Antifascist Protection
Wall' erected in 1961 by the
DDR to prevent the mass
exodus of its inhabitants.

★ Kollwitzplatz (B E2)
This pretty square at the
heart of Prenzlauer Berg is
less popular with the
alternative Berlin scene
since the façades regained
their stucco and pastel
hues, but it is still enjoyable
to sip a Berliner Weisse on

the terrace or in one of the
cafés on Husemannstr.
At the center of the square
stands the statue of Käthe
Kollwitz.

★ LSD Viertel (B E2)
An old bastion of
underground culture in
Prenzlauer Berg, its
nickname is taken from the
initials of its three main
streets: Lychener Str.,
Schliemannstr. and
Dunckerstr. The alternating
pattern of restored façades
and dilapidated buildings
reflects the profile of its
inhabitants, who are either
advocates of a quiet life or
young aficionados of the
countless bars in the area.

FERNSEHTURM

ALEXANDERPLATZ

VOLKSPARK FRIEDRICHSHAIN

★ Märkisches Museum (C B3)
→ *Am Köllnischen Park 5*
Tel. 30 86 60
Tue-Sun 10am–6pm
Although this building resembles a Gothic monastery, it was built in 1908 to house a museum. Its maze of rooms and corridors retrace the history and civilization of Berlin, from the first traces of prehistoric settlers to everyday life in the 19th century, including Gothic sculptures from the Marienkirche. Don't miss the stereoscopic photos of the Kaiserpanorama, dating from the late 19th century.

★ Marx-Engels-Forum (C A2)
→ *Karl-Liebknecht-Str., Spandauer Str., Rathausstr.*
Inaugurated in 1986 by Erich Honecker, this monument is dedicated to the 'fathers of socialism' – Marx and Engels – who are throwing a paternal glance toward the East. Nearby, a fresco celebrates the joys of socialism and decries the capitalist world.

★ Nikolaiviertel (C A3)
A maze of little streets and medieval houses dating back to... 1987! The tiny St Nicholas district was completely reconstructed (sometimes using concrete)

around the Nikolaikirche to celebrate the 750th anniversary of the foundation of Berlin. The Gothic nave of the oldest monument in the city (1230–1878) houses an annex of the Märkisches Museum. Nearby, the rococo balconies of the Ephraïm Palace (banker to Frederick II) are a reconstruction.

★ Rotes Rathaus (C A2)
→ *Spandauer Str. 100*
The brick-colored silhouette of the 'Red City Hall' (1869), an example of architectural eclecticism, draws its inspiration from Italian Romanesque: its belfry was modeled on the campanile

built by Giotto for the Duomo in Florence. It i surrounded by a terrac frieze that charts the h of Berlin up to the foundation of the Emp

★ Marienkirche (C A
→ *Spandauer Str. 100*
Daily 10am–6pm (tour at
One of Berlin's few remaining medieval buildings, St Mary's ch pioneered the use of Brandenburg brick (en 13th c.; pinnacle turret 1418). Inside, the stark walls, the rhythmic har of the vaults and the lig streaming through the windows enhance the exuberant fittings: the

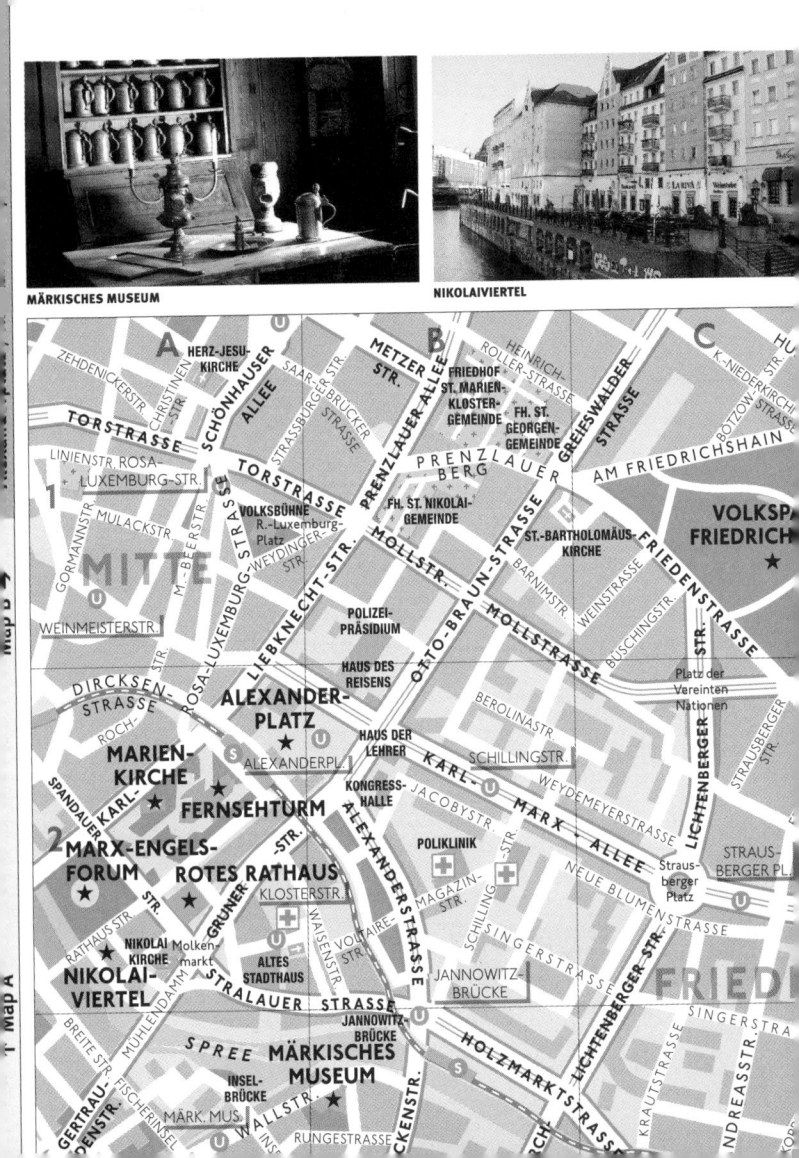

MÄRKISCHES MUSEUM

NIKOLAIVIERTEL

Map B

A   B   C

ZEHDENICKERSTR.
HERZ-JESU-KIRCHE
CHRISTINEN-STR.
SAAR-BRÜCKER-STR.
SCHÖNHAUSER ALLEE
STRASSBURGER STRASSE
METZER STR.
HEINRICH-ROLLER-STRASSE
FRIEDHOF ST. MARIEN-KLOSTER-GEMEINDE
FH. ST. GEORGEN-GEMEINDE
GREIFSWALDER STRASSE
K.-NIEDERKIRCH STR.
BÖTZOW STRASSE
HU

TORSTRASSE
LINIENSTR. ROSA-LUXEMBURG-STR.
TORSTRASSE
PRENZLAUER ALLEE
PRENZLAUER BERG
AM FRIEDRICHSHAIN

1

GORMANNSTR.
MULACKSTR.
M. BEERSTR.
ROSA-LUXEMBURG-STRASSE
VOLKSBÜHNE R.-Luxemburg-Platz
R.-Luxemburg-WEYDINGER-STR.
FH. ST. NIKOLAI-GEMEINDE
MÖLLSTR.
OTTO-BRAUN-STRASSE
ST.-BARTHOLOMÄUS-KIRCHE
FRIEDENSTRASSE
VOLKSPA FRIEDRICH ★

MITTE

WEINMEISTERSTR.
LIEBKNECHT-STR.
BARNIMSTR.
WEINSTRASSE
BÜSCHINGSTR.
LICHTENBERGER STR.
STRAUSBERGER STR.

DIRCKSEN-STRASSE
ROCH-STR.
POLIZEI-PRÄSIDIUM
MÖLLSTRASSE
BEROLINASTR.
Platz der Vereinten Nationen

ALEXANDER-PLATZ ★
HAUS DES REISENS
SCHILLINGSTR.

MARIEN-KIRCHE ★
SPANDAUER STR.
ALEXANDERPL. Ⓢ Ⓤ
HAUS DER LEHRER
KARL- Ⓤ MARX- Ⓤ ALLEE
WEYDEMEYERSTRASSE

FERNSEHTURM ★
KONGRESS-HALLE
JACOBYSTR.
Straus-berger Platz
STRAUS-BERGER PL. Ⓤ

2

KARL-STR.
MARX-ENGELS-FORUM ★
ALEXANDERSTRASSE
POLIKLINIK
SCHILLING-STR.
NEUE BLUMENSTRASSE

ROTES RATHAUS ★
GRUNER-STR.
KLOSTERSTR. Ⓤ ✚
MAGAZIN-STR.

RATHAUS STR.
NIKOLAI-KIRCHE ★
Molken-markt
ALTES STADTHAUS
VOLTAIRE-STR.
WAISENSTR.
JANNOWITZ-BRÜCKE
FRIEDI

NIKOLAI-VIERTEL
MÜHLENDAMM
STRALAUER STRASSE
JANNOWITZ-BRÜCKE Ⓤ
SINGERSTRA

BREITE STR.
FISCHERINSEL
SPREE
MÄRKISCHES MUSEUM ★
CKENSTR.
HOLZMARKTSTRASSE Ⓢ
LICHTENBERGER-STR.
SINGERSTRA

GERTRAU-DENSTR.
FISCHERINSEL
INSEL-BRÜCKE
MÄRK. MUS. Ⓤ
WALLSTR.
RUNGESTRASSE
KRAUTSTRASSE
NDREASSTRA

The 1,200ft-high television tower, a symbol of the former DDR, soars above a patchwork of architectural styles that reflect the successive political stances: the vast perspectives of the Stalinian Karl-Marx-Allee and the modernist buildings on Alexanderplatz, which stand next to the small studios in the St Nicholas district; this was entirely rebuilt in 1987. To the east, the gaily colored façades of the punk squats in Friedrichshain, with their alternative bars and clubs, and low rents, are turning Simon-Dach-Strasse into the new hub of the Berlin *Szene*.

SEASON

UMSPANNWERK OST

RESTAURANTS

Season (C A1)
→ *Rosa-Luxemburg-Str. 39*
Daily 10am–1am
A large traditional Berlin brasserie where you can warm yourself up with homemade mushroom soup at any time of the day. Dishes 3.50–10 €.

Sauerkraut und Bulgur (C D3)
→ *Strasse der Pariser Kommune 35*
Tel. 29 77 36 31
Daily 7.30am–midnight
A blend of Mediterranean and German tradition? A daring gamble... a winning gamble for these two young patrons bursting with ideas. Their restaurant stands out in sharp contrast to the solemnity of Karl-Marx-Allee. Dishes 6–10 €.

Umspannwerk Ost (C D2)
→ *Palisadenstr. 48*
Tel. 42 08 93 23
Daily 11.30am–midnight
This former factory now provides the setting for *nouvelle* cuisine. The dishes are served beneath steel vaults, delighting both your tastebuds and your wallet. The red tagliatelle with chicken, mushrooms and white wine sauce, are absolutely

divine. Dishes 9–13 €.

Alt-Berliner Wirtshaus Henne (C B4)
→ *Leuschnerdamm 25*
Tel. 614 77 30
Tue–Sun 7pm–midnight
Numerous specialties of roast chicken suggested by the restaurant's name. Rustic setting and terrace in summer. À la carte 12 €.

Lafil (C A1)
→ *Gormannstr. 22*
Tel. 285 990 26
Mon–Fri 1pm–1am;
Sat–Sun 4pm–1am
A taverna in Basque and Spanish colors that's always packed. Renowned for its *pinchos*, little skewers of meat and grilled vegetables, which are so tasty you don't need to be hungry to gorge on them. Dishes 7–15 €.

Zur letzten Instanz (C B3)
→ *Waisenstr. 14-16*
Tel. 242 55 28 Daily
noon–1am (11pm Sun)
The oldest *Kneipe* in Berlin (dating back to 1621) still has the remarkable heated seat on which Napoleon once sat when he lunched here. The restaurant serves a solid traditional style of cuisine: platter of assorted meats (with sauerkraut and *Kartoffeln*), or *Buletten*. Menu 9–11 €.

KAMMER

DIE TAGUNG

KAUFBAR

CAFÉS, BARS

Café Schönbrunn (C D1)
→ *Am Schwanenteich*
Volkspark Friedrichshain
Tel. 46 79 38 93
Daily 10pm–1am
By day a plain café-restaurant in the middle of Volkspark, where customers of all ages come to eat or take a break. By night a rather more fashionable bar with lounge music and a laid-back, youngish ambience.

Astrobar (C F4)
→ *Simon-Dach-Str. 40*
Daily from 6pm
Plastic astronauts and screens straight out of *Star Trek*: a cocktail bar in a spaceship. To withstand take-off you can sink into deep, low sofas, which make coming back down to earth a little tricky...

Dachkammer (C F4)
→ *Simon-Dach-Str. 39*
Tel. 296 16 73
Mon-Fri noon–2am;
Sat-Sun 10am–4am
A quieter, friendly *Kneipe*: good for a quiet chat over a drink. Wide selection of teas, all available in low-caffeine varieties.

Die Tagung (C F4)
→ *Wühlischstr. 29*
Tel. 292 87 56
Daily from 7pm
Ostalgie, red flags, busts of Lenin, official portraits and ensigns from the Communist Youth Movements are enjoying renewed popularity in Berlin, sometimes through genuine nostalgia, but often in mockery. The Tagung serves Roter Oktober, the beer once drunk by the crack corps of the Red Army. There's a club in the basement.

CLUBS, CONCERTS

Fischladen (C F2)
→ *Rigaer Str. 83*
Café: daily 5pm–3am
Club: Sat from 10pm
It can take over 15 minutes to walk through the four tiny rooms of this café-club, packed until 4am: two bars with 'destroy' decor, a reggae dance floor and another in the cellar, which is more of a dance-hall. Last but not least: the minuscule punk bar, where a hip crowd drinks beer, listens to reggae or trash-punk.

Maria am Ostbahnhof (C D4)
→ *An der Schillingbrücke 21*
Tel. 21 23 81 90
Fri-Sat from 11pm. Concerts during the week (from 8 or 9pm). www.clubmaria.de
This is the club for the techno avant-garde.

Excellent music and internationally renowned DJs.

Knorre (C F4)
→ *Revalerstr. 33*
Tel. 29 36 57 03
Daily from 6pm
www.knorre.de
A center for culture and arts: jazz, improvization theater, club...

Non Tox (C D4)
→ *Mühlenstr. 12*
Fri-Sat from 10pm; Sun 1pm
Decor reminiscent of a building site. Rock music and concerts, but a mixed crowd.

SHOPPING

c/o Alte Gerhardsen (C C3)
→ *Holtzmarktstr. 15-18*
Tel. 65 41 83 41
Tue-Sat 11am–6pm
This art gallery is worth a visit, less to buy, perhaps, than to witness the furious creative energy of modern Berlin. The exhibitions of installations and paintings are changed regularly.

Naturkost Friedrichshain (C F3)
→ *Boxhagenerstr. 109*
Tel. 29 66 04 52 Mon-Tue 9am–6.30pm; Sat 9am–1pm
This organic supermarket has a very wide choice of produce at prices that even beat the major supermarkets. The secret of its success, however, is its bread counter with amazing fresh produce.

Prachtmädchen (C F4)
→ *Wühlischstr. 28*
Tel. 97 00 27 80 Mon-Fri 11am–8pm; Sat 11am–4pm
With 1930s decor for a chic and engaging style (mainly in muddy purples and sky blue colors). Striped tights and flowery boots: it's spring all year here!

Kaufbar (C F4)
→ *Gärtnerstr. 4*
Tel. 29 77 88 25
Daily 11am–1am
People come here to drink a cup of tea, and end up buying the cup. This is more than just a bar: it's a bar-cum-second-hand shop, where everything that you see here can either be consumed or purchased.

Chapati Design (C F4)
→ *Simon-Dach-Str. 37-38*
Tel. 29 04 40 23 Mon-Sat 11am–8pm (5pm Sat)
On the left, a completely handmade ready-to-wear fashion in a hippie chic style that displays an Indian inspiration: velvet flares, gold-embroidered shawls. On the right, crafts imported direct from Azerbaijan and the Maghreb: Persian rugs, kilims and glassware.

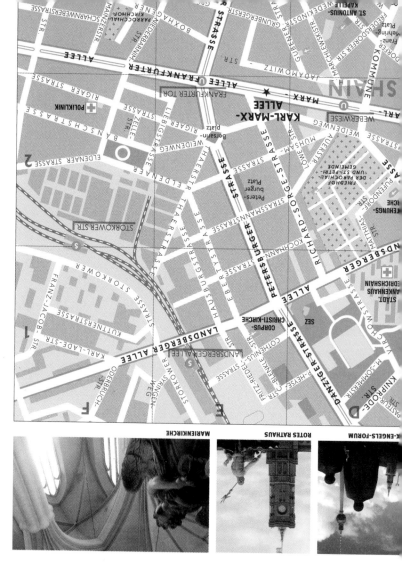

MARIENKIRCHE

ROTES RATHAUS

X-ENGELS-FORUM

-MARX-ALLEE

EAST SIDE GALLERY

que pulpit by Andreas
üter (1703) and the
n by J. Wagner (recitals
30pm on Sat, May-Oct).
e left of the entrance is
h-century Dance of
h (visit Mon-Tue 1pm).

ernsehturm (C A2)
l 242 33 33
h-Oct: daily 9am–1am
ascent midnight). Nov-
daily 10am–midnight
ascent 11.30pm)
ole from all of Berlin, the
o-foot-high spire of the
vision Tower, built in
9, defined West
many from its dizzy
hts. There is a fabulous
v from the panoramic
form and the revolving

restaurant, housed in the
steel sphere at 666 feet.
★ **Alexanderplatz (C** A2)
Despite its gigantic
proportions, the 'Alex' is still
the true hub of East Berlin.
Completely bombed, the
working-class counterpart of
Potsdamer Platz made way,
in the 1960s, for a huge
esplanade surrounded by
concrete blocks. At the
center stands the World
Time Clock by Erich John,
and a fountain of the
Friendships of Peoples.
★ **Volkspark
Friedrichshain (C** D1)
Behind the neo-Baroque
Fairy Tale fountain (1913)
and its statues taken from

Grimm, stretch the woods
and grass of the People's
Park (1840). In summer,
Berliners flock here to
sunbathe. In winter, the two
hills, made from debris from
a bombed bunker and local
landfill, are used as
toboggan runs. This is the
burial place of 200 victims
of the 1848 revolution.
★ **Karl-Marx-Allee (C** E3)
The asphalt of the former
Stalineallee is tank-proof:
the massive parades from
the East used to rumble up
this colossal avenue to
reach Alexanderplatz. The
building of the historicist-
Stalinian buildings on this
'Moscow-on-the-Spree' gave

rise, on June 17, 1953,
to a workers' revolt, which
was violently put down
to prevent it spreading
throughout the city.
★ **East Side Gallery (C** D4)
→ *Mühlenstr.*
www.eastsidegallery.com
Stretching for over
4,265 feet, this is the
world's longest outdoor
art gallery. In 1990, 106
artists used the East side
of the Wall as a vast blank
page. Fresco after fresco
has created a cavalcade
of colors. Damaged by the
weather and by tourists
who try to pull away
fragments, they are slowly
being restored.

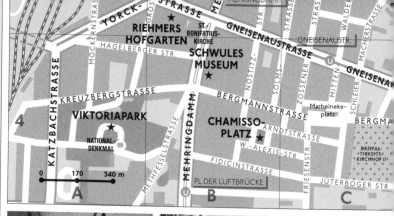

KÜNSTLERHAUS BETHANIEN

SCHWULES MUSEUM

RIEHMERS HOFGARTEN

★ Haus am Checkpoint Charlie (D B1)

→ *Friedrichstr. 43-45*
Tel. 253 72 50
Daily 9am–10pm

On the site of the crossing point between the American and Soviet sectors, this museum presents a chronological history of the Wall with accounts by defectors and the amazing stratagems some used successfully to escape, such as hiding in suitcases. On the top floor, there is an exhibition on non-violence.

★ Stiftung Topographie des Terrors (D B1)

→ *Niederkirchnerstr. 8*
Tel. 254 86 703 Daily
10am–8pm (6pm Oct-April)

The sinister headquarters of the Third Reich (Gestapo, secret services, Waffen SS) stood on this piece of wasteland until 1945. The foundations of underground cells, uncovered in 1987, now house an exhibition on Nazism and deportation.

★ Martin Gropius Bau (D A1)

→ *Niederkirchnerstr. 7*
Tel. 25 48 60
Wed–Mon 10am–8pm

When building the School of Applied Arts (1887–91), Schmiede and Gropius took a leaf out of Schinkel's book: neo-Renaissance eclecticism and graceful decoration (ceramics and mosaics). The building is now used for major exhibitions.

★ Jüdisches Museum (D C2)

→ *Lindenstr. 9-14*
Tel. 25 993 300 Daily
10am–8pm (10pm Mon)
www.jmberlin.de

The symbolic, 'deconstructivist' structure of this building by Daniel Libeskind (1999), which is shaped like an exploded Jewish star, attracted hundreds of thousands of visitors long before any exhibits were brought inside the museum. The focus of the permanent exhibition is on the historical role of the Jewish community right its annihilation by the N

★ Künstlerhaus Bethanien (D F2)

→ *Mariannenplatz 2*
Tel. 616 90 30
Wed–Sun 2–7pm

This is an art center in a 19th-century hospital, where, leading off the h neo-Romanesque foyer, a maze of spotless whit rooms and corridors ope onto exhibitions of mod art. Each artist is given a studio for a year for the purpose of creating a w that will be exhibited aft their stay. In summer, th is an open-air movie the behind the building.

Flanked by the Wall on two sides and therefore abandoned by the *Wessis* investors, Kreuzberg was the haunt of dropouts, Turkish laborers and young rebels until 1989. Punks and pacifists flocked here from all over West Germany to avoid military service, and they created new lifestyles and new types of militant activity in alternative communities. They have now taken refuge in Friedrichshain and, although the area around Kottbusser Tor continues to look like a little Istanbul, the western part of the district is particularly delightful for its ancient façades clustered around Viktoriapark.

AL KALIF

GOLGATHA

RESTAURANTS

Curry 36 (D B3)
→ *Mehringdamm 36*
Mon-Fri 9am–4am; Sat 10am–4am; Sun 11am–4am
A grilled sausage smothered in ketchup and curry, or in a *Brötchen*, with onions (*Zwiebeln*) – fantastic Berlin specialties.

Al Kalif (D C4)
→ *Bergmannstr. 105*
Tel. 694 47 34
Daily noon–midnight
Take a relaxing break in Palestine: remove your shoes when you go in and stretch out on the rugs and cushions. Excellent home-made dishes prepared using fresh produce. Couscous, hummus and falafel, served with mocha café or cinnamon tea – no alcohol. Dishes 4–7.50 €.

Osteria no. 1 (D A4)
→ *Kreuzbergstr. 71*
Tel. 786 91 62
Daily noon–midnight
Kreuzbergstrasse is Berlin's Little Italy and Osterie no. 1 a warm, classy, good-value Italian restaurant, which has swiftly become extremely popular. Generous portions and attractively presented dishes – *vitello tonnato* (minced veal in tuna and caper sauce), pasta, pizza, *saltimbocca*.

Reservation advised. Dishes 8–16 €.

Austria (D C4)
→ *Bergmannstr. 30*
Tel. 694 44 40 Daily 6pm–1am (7pm June-Aug)
A traditional Austrian *Gaststätte*, renowned for the quality of its cooking: *Wienerschnitzel* and *Strudel* of course, but also many other specialties. Reservation necessary. Dishes 12–17 €.

Ramses Café Restaurant (D A1)
→ *Stresemannstr. 128*
Tel. 22 65 11 20 Mon-Sat noon–11pm; Sun 1–11pm
Classic Egyptian cuisine, with a few original international dishes; very good wine list with French, Lebanese and Spanish labels. Menu 20 €.

Altes Zollhaus (D D3)
→ *Carl-Herz-Ufer 30*
Tel. 692 33 00
Tue-Sat 6–11pm
One of the best restaurants in Berlin, in a half-timbered tavern on the banks of the canal. Light, innovative German cuisine prepared with the finest produce. The Brandenburg duck *magret* with mashed potato and cabbage is delicious. Superb wine list, ranging from ordinary pitchers to bottles of Romanée-Conti. Menu 35–50 €.

KLAUSE

LE BATEAU IVRE　　　　**FASTER PUSSYCAT**

BIERGARTEN, CAFÉS

Café Adler (D A4)
→ *Friedrichstr. 206*
Tel 251 89 65 Mon-Sat
10am–midnight (7pm Sun)
Overlooking the old
Checkpoint Charlie (hence
its fame and popularity)
is the small, atmospheric,
chic and slightly faded
Café Adler. It serves
German and continental
cooking, but you can go for
just a coffee or a beer. It is
easy to see why John Le
Carré (Tom Clancy too,
apparently) stopped by so
often. Menu 18 €.

Golgatha (D A4)
→ *Katzbachstr.,*
Viktoriapark (opposite the
football pitch) Tel 785 24 53
April-Sep: daily 10–6am
The Golgatha *Biergarten*,
at the foot of the
Kreuzberg, is one of the
most famous of the 'beer
gardens' that flourish in
summer on sidewalks and
in parks. On Sat and Sun,
it transforms into a club
and concert venue.

Locus (D C4)
→ *Marheinekeplatz 4*
Tel. 69 156 37
Daily 10am–1.30am
Enjoy a hearty *Frühstück*,
away from the hustle and
bustle of the market.
With classical music in the
background and, in

summer, a pretty terrace
overlooking the square.

Ankerklause (D F3)
→ *Kottbusserbrücke 1*
Tel. 693 56 49
Mon 4pm–5am;
Tue-Sun 10am–5am
On the banks of the
Landwehrkanal, this white
and blue café, resembling
a barge, is a pleasant spot
in the afternoon. Later,
it is crowded with people
enjoying easy-listening
tracks on the jukebox.

Le Bateau Ivre (D F2)
→ *Oranienstr. 18*
Tel. 61 40 36 59
Daily 9am–3am
Talking at the bar or
debating under the
lanterns, a cultured and
fashionable clientele
gather here, and the café
is always rammed. You
might even bump into a
German movie star.

CLUBS, CONCERTS

Schnabelbar (D E2)
→ *Oranienstr. 31*
Tel. 615 35 34
Daily from 9pm
Soft lighting and stylish
semi-ethnic, semi-
industrial decor: a typical
cocktail bar for trendy
Kreuzberg. Evenings, DJs
mix house music (Wed, Fri
and Sat), techno (Tue) or
Latino (Mon).

SO 36 (D F2)
→ *Oranienstr. 199*
Tel. 61 40 13 06
Daily: call for info on
concerts. www.so36.de
One of the most
unmissable concert
venues and clubs on the
Berlin scene. Eclectic
programs: hip-hop,
ballroom dancing (Sun
6pm, 7pm in summer),
house music evenings for
lesbians (Wed) or for the
inveterate survivors of the
weekend (Mon).

SAUNA

**Liquidrom
Therme (D** A2)
→*Möckernstr. 10*
Tel. 74 73 71 71
Sun-Tue 10am–10pm;
Fri- Sat 10am–midnight
(2am on the full moon)
Enough sightseeing? Enjoy
a dry or humid sauna, an
outdoor jacuzzi, refreshing
fruit cocktails and, best of
all, a warm seawater bath
with aquatic music and
subdued lighting. Note
that in Germany, saunas
are mixed and often nude.

SHOPPING

Faster Pussycat (D B4)
→ *Mehringdamm 57*
Tel. 69 50 66 00
Mon-Fri 11am–8pm; Sat

11am–6pm
The best of stylish Berlin:
retro but not backward.
New-style wigs and retro
coats vie for attention.

Colours (D B4)
→ *Bergmannstr. 102*
(rear of the courtyard, 1st floor
on the right) Tel 694 33 48
Mon-Sat 11am–7pm
(6pm Sat)
This remarkable second-
hand clothes supermarket
sells everything: from
classic jeans to wild
psychedelic dresses,
mini-skirts and T-shirts.

**Markthalle
Kreuzberg (D** C4)
→ *Bergmannstr., Zossener*
Str. Mon-Fri 7am–8pm;
Sat 7am–4pm
You can find everything
in this tower of Babel:
underwear and cigars,
Turkish and Greek
specialties, fresh produce
and even animals! Built in
1822, the market hall is
without doubt *the* meeting
place of the area.

Kadò (D E3)
→ *Graefestr. 75*
Tel. 69 04 16 38
Tue-Fri 9.30am–6.30pm;
Sat 9am–2pm
An old, quaint little grocer's
store, where everything is
made from liquorice!
Sweet, salty or tangy, you
inevitably leave with your
cone; from 100g at 1.20 €.

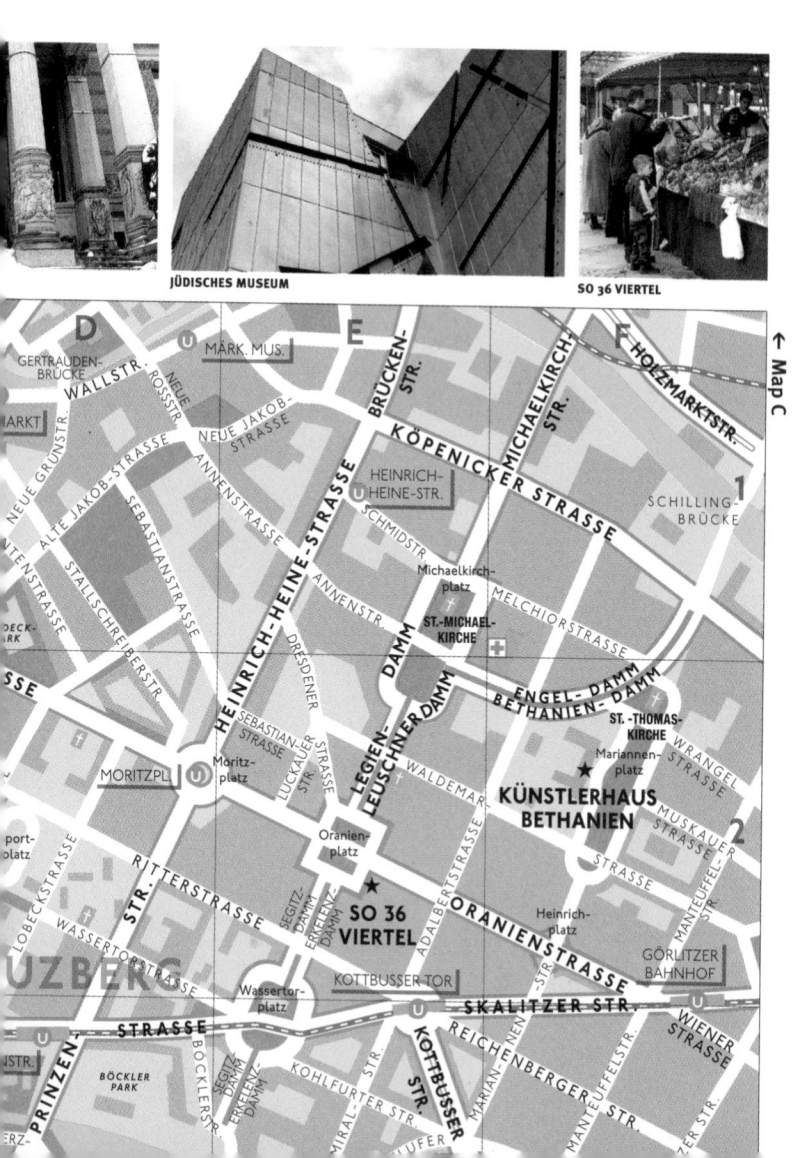

JÜDISCHES MUSEUM

SO 36 VIERTEL

← Map C

D
E
F

GERTRAUDEN-BRÜCKE

WALLSTR.

MÄRK. MUS.

MARKT

NEUE GRÜNSTR.

ROSSTR.

ALTE JAKOB-STRASSE

NEUE JAKOB-STRASSE

SEBASTIANSTRASSE

STALLSCHREIBERSTR.

ANNENSTRASSE

BRÜCKEN-STR.

MICHAELKIRCH-STR.

HOLZMARKTSTR.

KÖPENICKER STRASSE

HEINRICH-HEINE-STR.

SCHMIDSTR.

SCHILLING-BRÜCKE

1

ANNENSTR.

Michaelkirch-platz

ST.-MICHAEL-KIRCHE

MELCHIORSTRASSE

DECK-PARK

DRESDENER

HEINRICH-HEINE-STRASSE

DAMM

ENGEL-DAMM

BETHANIEN-DAMM

ST.-THOMAS-KIRCHE

SEBASTIAN-STRASSE

LEGIEN-LEUSCHNERDAMM

WALDEMAR

Mariannen-platz

WRANGEL-STRASSE

MORITZPL.

Moritz-platz

LUCKAUER STRASSE

KÜNSTLERHAUS BETHANIEN

MUSKAUER STRASSE

port-platz

Oranien-platz

ADALBERTSTRASSE

STRASSE

MANTEUFFEL-

RITTERSTRASSE

SO 36 VIERTEL

ORANIENSTRASSE

LÜBECKSTRASSE

STR.

SEGITZ-DAMM

ERICLENZ-DAMM

Heinrich-platz

GÖRLITZER BAHNHOF

WASSERTOR-

UZBERG

KOTTBUSSER TOR

Wassertor-platz

SKALITZER STR.

STRASSE

BÖCKLER PARK

BÖCKLERSTR.

PRINZEN-

SEGITZ-DAMM

ERICLENZ-DAMM

KOHLFURTER STR.

KOTTBUSSER STR.

REICHENBERGER

WIENER STRASSE

NSTR.

MIRAL-NEN-

MARIAN-NEN-

UFER

MANTEUFFELSTR.

2

VIKTORIAPARK

CHAMISSOPLATZ

36 Viertel (D E2)
...rmer 'Süd-Ost 36' is
...ub of working-class
...berg. The traditional
...demonstrations
...ss the political
...ement of some of the
...ct's inhabitants.
...st of the year, life
...ves quietly around the
...ets (Kottbusser Tor and
...zer Park), the *Imbiss*,
...sh grocery stores
...ienstr. and Kottbusser
...n) and along the
...wehrkanal.

**hwules
...eum (D** B4)
...hringdamm 61
...9 59 90 50
...Mon 2–6pm (7pm Sat)

Before the Nazis, Berlin was
home to the largest gay
community in Europe. After
the war, although in West
Germany *Schwule* and
Lesben regrouped in
Schöneberg, East Berlin
remained the only city in
East Germany where they
were tolerated. Apart from
the exhibitions put on by
the gay museum, there is
a richly stocked library.

**★ Riehmers
Hofgarten (D** B3)
→ *Between Grossbeerenstr.,
Yorckstr. & Hagelberger Str.*
Neo-Renaissance façades
facing wide tree-lined
avenues: this is how 19th-
century Berlin should have

looked. The 328-foot-long
plots of land provided by
James Hobrecht in his plan
(1856) were to have been
reached by small inner
streets. To cut costs, the
developers crowded the
cramped rental apartment
blocks (*Mietskasernen*)
around small dark
courtyards. Only Wilhelm
Riehmer did differently.

★ Viktoriapark (D A4)
This neo-Romantic park
laid out on the highest
hill in Berlin (1888–94) is
topped by the National
Monument, which
commemorates the war
of liberation against
Napoleon. The Gothic

spire built by Schinkel
(1817–21) is graced by an
iron cross (*Kreuz*) from
which the district took its
name. To the north, a man-
made waterfall cascades
down the hill over concrete
rocks and beneath bridges
made of imitation wood.

★ Chamissoplatz (D B4)
→ *Organic market here on
Sat 8am–2pm*
This is probably the most
typical square of pre-war
Berlin: the *Mietskasernen*
retain their delicately hued
neo-Renaissance façades
and the small square still
has its turn-of-the-century
urinals: a miracle in this
badly bombed area.

GEMÄLDEGALERIE

NEUE NATIONALGALERIE

★ Hamburger Bahnhof Museum für Gegenwart Berlin (E D1)

→ *Invalidenstr. 50-51*
Tel. 397 8340 Tue-Fri 10am–6pm; Sat-Sun 11am–6pm
This museum of modern art is in the city's oldest railway station (1847). The metal structure of the vast hall and the side wings, renovated by Kleihues, provide a fitting arena for installations by Beuys and artworks by Warhol.

★ Reichstag (E D2)

→ *Platz der Republik 1*
Tel. 22 73 21 52 Mon-Fri 9am–5pm (6pm in summer); Sat-Sun and public hols 10am–4pm (9am–6pm in summer).
Dome: daily 8am–10pm

Built in 1894, the building witnessed the death throes of the Weimar Republic before being torched by the Nazis on Feb 27, 1933. A symbol of the fall of Berlin, it was not until reunification that it welcomed the Bundestag under its new glass cupola (Norman Foster, 1999). Solemn and imposing, it attracts many strollers who've come to enjoy its esplanade.

★ Potsdamer Platz (E D4)

The biggest crossroads in Europe and the heart of the residential city in the 1920s, this square was razed to the ground by bombs. In the past ten years, this vast wasteland, bisected by the Wall, has become a flourishing business center.

Sony Center

www.sonycenter.de
The headquarters of Sony Europe, designed by Helmut Jahn. Beneath the vast tent over the buildings, light plays with the water features, next to the neo-Baroque vestiges of the Grandhotel Esplanade, which was put onto jacks and air cushions and moved aside so that the Center could be built.

★ Gemäldegalerie (E C4)

→ *Kulturforum, Matthaikirchplatz 4*
Tel. 266 29 51 Tue-Sun 10am–6pm (10pm Thu).
In the naturally lit rooms of

the Kulturforum (1998 Caravaggio follows Gic and Cranach follows V Eyck for a comprehens overview of 13th- to 18 century European pair Sadly, some 400 canv from the Hohenzollern huge collection were l during the bombing of Friedrichshain bunker. Next door, there is a fir museum of decorative from the Middle Ages present day.

★ Neue Nationalgalerie (E C.

→ *Kulturforum, Potsdam*
Tel. 266 2951
Tue-Fri 10am–6pm (10pm Thu); Sat-Sun 11am–6pm
Picasso, Ernst, De Chir

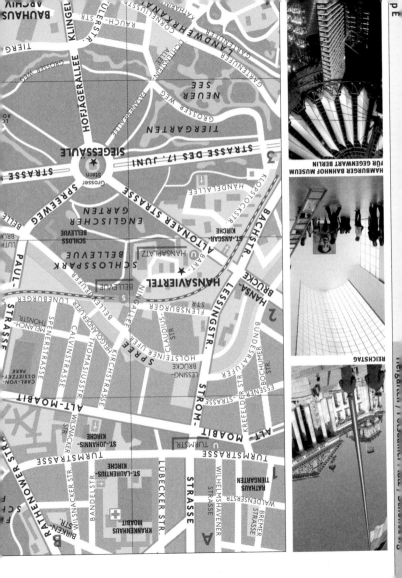

Surrounding the Siegessäule and the Schloss Bellevue, now the president's home, the Tiergarten, former hunting preserve of the Hohenzollerns, is a cool oasis of greenery in the city and a popular destination for summer barbecues. Further south, the buildings on the new Potsdamer Platz form an extension of the Kulturforum and serve as a monument to leading contemporary architects. By comparison, the peaceful Schöneberg district appears extremely unassuming. However, appearances can be deceptive: the gay community parties into the early hours of the morning in the many bars and clubs.

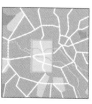

KAISERSAAL

HAKUIN

RESTAURANTS

Goltzstrasse (E B6)
Schöneberg's restaurant-lined street.
Shayan
→ *Goltzstr. 23 Tel. 215 15 47*
Daily noon–midnight
A welcoming family atmosphere and very good Indo-Iranian cuisine. Dishes 4.50–15 €.
Indischer Imbiss
→ *Goltzstr. 33*
Tel. 215 49 65 Daily 11am–1am (2am Fri-Sat)
This restaurant's kitsch decor must be seen: a Hindu altar, incense, glitzy statuettes, hangings and garlands of lights. Healthy food and generous portions. Dishes 5 €.
Tiergartenquelle (E A3)
→ *Bachstr. 6 (under the Tiergarten subway station) Tel. 392 76 15*
Daily noon–midnight
Near Hansaplatz, this friendly, family-run *Kneipe* is located under the arches of the S-Bahnhof Tiergarten. Traditional German cuisine: platter of cooked meats, Nuremberg sauerkraut or escalopes. Dishes 6–10 €.
Pan y Tulipan (E C5)
→ *Winterfeldstr. 40*
Tel. 21 91 30 14 Daily 10am (9am Sat)–midnight
A very warm and friendly

service – you can't help but smile back, and Spanish cuisine in generous portions. There's a lounge on the first floor for more intimate meals on snug sofas. Dishes 8–16 €.
Alte Pumpe (E B6)
→ *Lützowstr. 42*
Tel. 26 48 42 65
Mon-Sat 11am–midnight; Sun 10am–4pm
High-quality German cuisine in a former factory, with a gigantic diesel-powered water pump, from the 1920s, providing a focus for the decoration. Brunch on Sun (10 €) and jazz concerts on Wed night. Menu 16 €.
Café Einstein (E B5)
→ *Kufürstenstr. 58*
Tel. 261 50 96
Daily 9am–midnight
A faultless classic: Austrian cuisine in a *Jugendstil* villa. In summer *Wiener Schnitzel* and Viennese cafés are served in the garden. À la carte 30 €.
Dachgarten (E D2)
→ *Platz der Republik*
Tel. 226 299 33
Daily 9am–5pm, 6.30pm–midnight
Restaurant on the roof of the Reichstag with some good German dishes enhanced by fantastic views over the city. Reservation is essential

PELNEST 3000

PHILHARMONIE

DECO ARTS

and will allow you to jump the queue for Norman Foster's 1999 dome. À la carte 30 €.

Hakuin (E A5)
→ Martin-Luther-Str. 1
Tel. 218 20 27 Tue-Sat 5–11.30pm; Sun noon–11.30pm
Welcome to this Asian oasis: plants and an indoor fountain, Zen music and subdued lighting. One of the best (if not *the* best) vegetarian restaurants in Berlin. Expensive. Dishes 20–30 €.

Kaisersaal (E D4)
→ Potsdamerplatz
Tel. 261 50 96
Daily 9am–midnight.
www.kaisersaal-berlin.de
Royal cuisine at the Emperor's table, in the former Grandhotel Esplanade. These historic 'salons', or dining rooms, at the heart of the ultra-modern Potsdamer Platz are now one of Berlin's most fashionable meeting places. Menus 50–80 €.

CAFÉS, BARS

Walhalla (E A1)
→ Krefelderstr. 6 (corner of Essenerstr.) Tel. 393 3039
Daily 10am–2am
www.walhalla-berlin.de
This *Kneipe* is always full: it has a pool table, a

terrace looking onto the street when the weather is good, some good dishes and fine beers, i.e. all the right things to make it a favorite among locals.

Café M (E B6)
→ Goltzstr. 33
Tel. 216 7092 Mon-Fri 8am–2am; Sat-Sun 9am–3am
Lively mixed bar (straight and gay), with a background of electronic and jungle music. Drink white russians, mojitos or beers.

Joseph Roth Diele (E C5)
→ Potsdamerstr. 75
Mon-Fri 10am–midnight
Office workers, labourers, students and passersby come here for the famous *Gulashsuppe*. An old taverna in which there is always someone keen to play a tune on the piano.

CONCERT HALL, THEATER

Philharmonie (E D4)
→ Herbert-von-Karajan-Str. 1
Tel. 25 4880 (general info).
Ticket office: Mon-Fri 3–6pm; Sat-Sun 11am–2pm.
www.berlin-philharmonic.com
The illustrious Berliner Philharmonisches Orchester make the most of the superb acoustics in the huge amphitheater-

shaped auditorium, one of the finest concert halls in the world, designed by Hans Scharoun. There is also chamber music at the Kammermusiksaal.

Grips Theater (E A2)
→ Altonaer Str. 22 (Hansaplatz) Tel. 39 74 7477
Ticket office: Mon-Fri noon–6pm; Sat-Sun 11am–5pm.
www.grips-theater.de
People of all ages pack into this amphitheater-style auditorium. Plays by the Grips company – politically committed yet good-natured – provide musical thumbnail sketches of Berlin life, such as the legendary *Line 1*.

SHOPPING

Garage (E B5)
→ Ahornstr. 2 Tel. 211 27 60
Mon-Fri 11am–7pm (8pm Thu-Fri); Sat 11am–6pm
This store has the cheapest second-hand clothes in the city, but not always the latest fashions. Everything is sold by weight: 7 €/ lb.

Deco Arts (E B6)
→ Motzstr. 6
Tel. 21 586 72 Wed-Fri 3–6.30pm; Sat 11am–3pm
This store specializes in 20th-century furniture and decoration: Verner Panton lamps, Breuyers

armchairs, English sofas, as well as pretty vases, accessories and unusual articles.

Antike Möbel (E B6)
→ Goltzstr. 49
Tel. 216 37 19 Mon-Fri 1–7pm; Sat 10am–3pm
This antiques dealer and restorer has some fine pieces of German antique furniture. He also sells beeswax candles made using traditional methods.

Harb (E C5)
→ Potsdamer Str. 93
Tel. 261 19 36 Mon-Fri 9am–7.30pm; Sat 9am–2pm
An Ali Baba's cave full of exquisite crockery, lamps, music, incense and teas. For the gourmets: fresh olives and dried fruits, marinaded vegetables and Oriental pâtisserie.

CLUB

Kumpelnest 3000 (E C5)
→ Lützowstr. 23
Tel. 261 69 18 Daily 11pm–5am (11am Fri-Sat)
Ultra-kitsch decor and music: the barman is an expert on the Deutsche Schlager – schmaltzy German songs from the 1970s – and he also knows the 50 most recent winners of the Eurovision Song Contest by heart. Laid-back and friendly atmosphere.

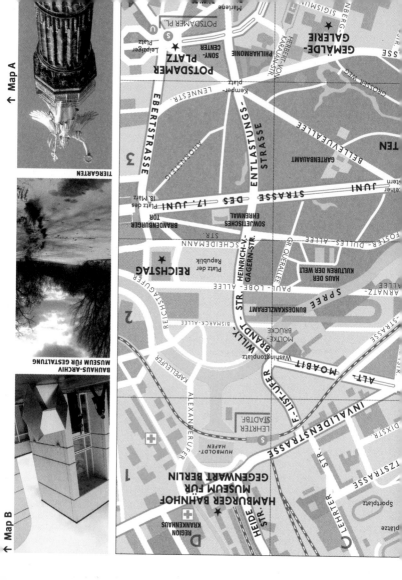

HANSAVIERTEL

SCHÖNEBERG

glasshouse for modern [b]uilt by Mies van der [...]e in 1968, has a large [...]essionist section: [...]schka and Munch, and [...]nan painters from Die [...]ke (Kirchner, Nolde) [...]Die Neue Sachlichkeit [...]w reality') – Dix, Grosz [...]Beckmann.

auhaus Archiv-Museum Gestaltung (E B4)
ingelhöferstr. 14
54 00 20
-Mon 10am–5pm
tionalism, rejection of mentation and netrization: the building structed in 1979 to plans alter Gropius applies ciples advocated by the haus, which Gropius ran

from 1919 to 1932. The museum exhibits paintings and models by artists from this school, which united art, design and architecture: Kandinsky, Breuyer, etc.

★ Tiergarten (E A3)
This green lung of 412 acres, in the heart of the city, is the old hunting reserve of the Hohenzollerns. It transforms into a huge barbecue in summer. The park houses the Schloss Bellevue and the House of World Culture, architectural testament to the 1950s.

★ Siegessäule (E B3)
→ *Strasse des 17. Juni*
Daily 9.30am–6.30pm (7pm Fri-Sun); Nov-March: 9.30am–5.30pm (6pm Fri-Sun)

From the top of its 194ft-high pedestal decorated with cannons taken from Prussia's enemies, 'Goldelse' watches over the Tiergarten. The golden angel from Wim Wenders' *Wings of Desire* commemorates Prussia's victories over Denmark (1864), Austria (1866) and France (1871). Originally set up opposite the Reichstag, it was moved here by Hitler in 1938. There are breathtaking panoramic views from the top.

★ Hansaviertel (E A2)
→ *Hansaplatz Project*
In 1953, as a counterpart to the building sites on Karl-Marx-Allee, West Berlin commissioned 48 architects

(Gropius, Niemeyer, Aalto...) to build 1,400 apartments. These apartment blocks, scattered amidst greenery around a store-lined square, marked the apex of the town-planning projects developed in Berlin as a reaction to the *Mietskasernen*.

★ Schöneberg (E B6)
The ageing façades and modern buildings in this charming little residential district are home to one of the largest gay communities in Europe. In the trendy bars on Goltzstrasse and the surrounding area, no one bats an eyelid at the prominent number of gay and lesbian couples.

SAMMLUNG BERGGRUEN

ÄGYPTISCHES MUSEUM

★ Kaiser-Wilhelm-Gedächtniskirche (F E3)
→ *Breitscheidplatz*
Tel 218 50 23
Mon-Sat 10am-4pm.
Church: daily 9am-7pm
Since 1943, this 'Memorial church' (1890–5) has been pointing its damaged steeple skyward, reminding passersby of the wreckage caused by the bombings (over a third of the city's houses were destroyed). At night, the tower and nave of the new church (1961) form two prisms of blue glass illuminated from within.

★ Savignyplatz (F D3)
A 'forest' of parasols surrounds large, peaceful, tree-lined streets with Jugendstil façades. Late into the night, lively cafés are packed with students from the nearby universities.

★ Zoologischer Garten (F F3)
→ *Budapester Str. 34*
Tel 25 40 10 Daily
9am-6.30pm (5pm winter)
Bison wander around an Indian totem pole, the giraffe house is reminiscent of a mosque and the mouflon enclosure resembles an alpine crest. Behind its pagoda-like entrance gate the Lenné Zoo (1844), with 15,000 animals (including two pandas), is one of the world's largest.

★ Käthe-Kollwitz-Museum (F D4)
→ *Fasanenstr. 24*
Tel. 882 52 10
Wed-Mon 11am-6pm
The Expressionist work of Käthe Kollwitz (1867–1945) conveys her horror at the poverty she discovered with her husband, a doctor, in Prenzlauer Berg. As most of her sculptures were destroyed during World War Two, the museum largely exhibits her engravings.

★ Bröhan-Museum (F A2)
→ *Schloss-Str. 10*
Tel. 32 69 06 00
Tue-Sun 10am-6pm
Gallé vases, porcelain from Copenhagen, furniture by Guimard, Van de Velde Ruhlmann. Karl H. Bröh collection, devoted to designs from 1889 to 19 features the virtuoso arabesques of Jugends and the spare lines of Art Deco.

★ Sammlung Berggruen (F A1)
→ *Schloss-Str. 1*
Tue-Sun 10am-6pm
The greatest names in modern art collected by Heinz Berggruen, a shre gallery owner: Cézanne, Matisse, Giacometti, Kl Over 80 works spanning Picasso's entire career, the Blue period to the w

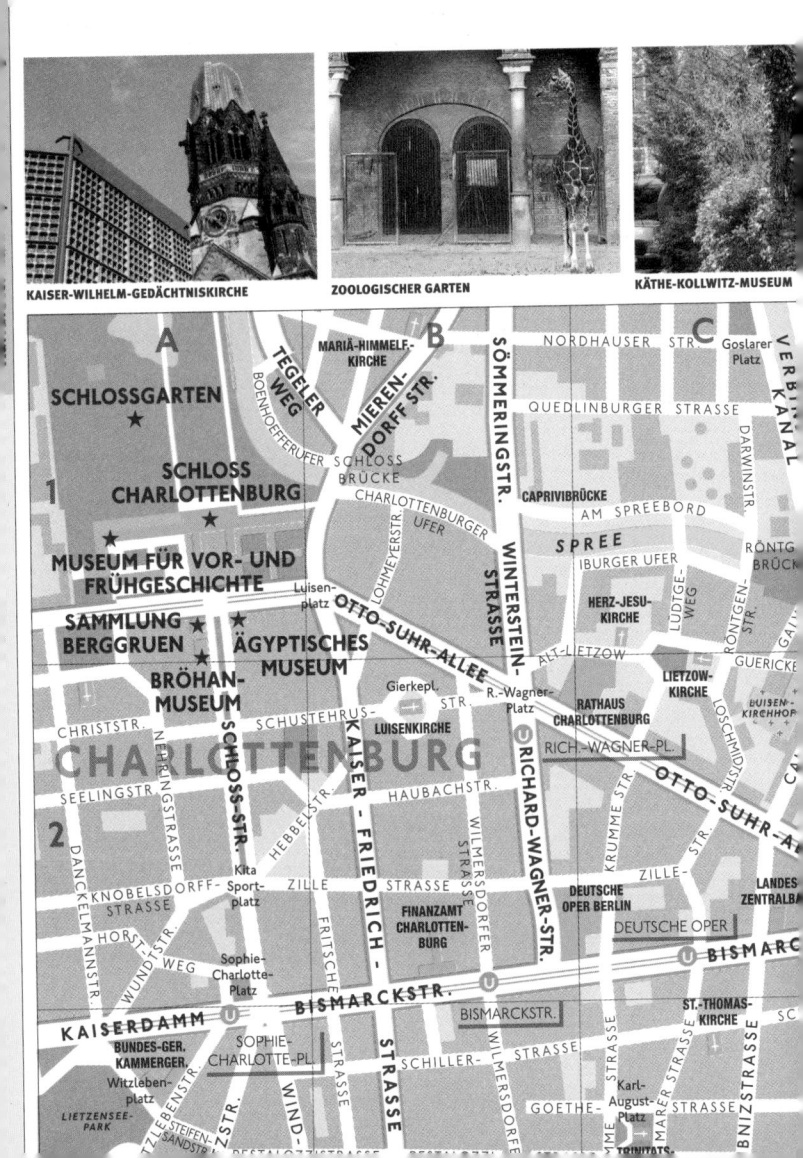

The 'Ku'Damm', at the center of West Berlin, is like a capitalist Unter den Linden. Today, where cabarets and cafés once drew a bohemian crowd in the 1920s, a string of rather characterless buildings houses a variety of stores owned by large international fashion brands. However, even since the fall of the Wall, droves of tourists and Berliners continue to take the district's main thoroughfares to the shops and theaters. Further west, the middle-class residences of Charlottenburg – small apartment blocks and luxury villas – cluster around the Baroque castle and its adjoining museums.

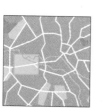

DAO THAÏ

CAFE IM LITERATURHAUS

RESTAURANTS

Dao Thaï (F C3)
→ *Kantstr. 133*
Tel. 37 59 14 14
Daily 11am–2am
Casseroles simmer behind the counter: Thai specialties served directly from the pan to your plate. Dishes 5–12 €.

**Le Savoie Rire/
Ty Breizh (F** C3)
→ *Tegerleweg 104*
Tel. 345 60 155
Daily 5pm–1am
For the past 23 years, the Savoyard Patrick Mattei has been running a Breton bistro... in Berlin! Come here for loud conversation, merry laughter and hits by singers Reggiani or Ferré, sung by diners at the top of their voices. Excellent wine list and varied cheeses from the Savoie region. Menu 12 €.

**Cafe im
Literaturhaus (F** D4)
→ *Fasanenstr. 23*
Tel 882 54 14
Daily 9.30am–1am
Fine gravel paths winding through lawns and banks of flowers, a Jugendstil glasshouse made of wrought iron, and staff dressed in white suits with bow-ties: take a break from the frenetic activity of the Ku'Damm to recall

what it was like when people took their time. Global cuisine and a good wine list. Dishes 15–25 €.

Good Friends (F C3)
→ *Kantstr. 30*
Tel. 313 26 59
Daily noon–2am
The waiters are in a constant flurry as they glide through three lively dining rooms. More than 100 dishes are on offer at this hangout of Berlin's Chinese community. Dishes 7–14 €

Scarabeo (F D4)
→ *Ludwigkirchstr. 6*
Tel. 885 06 16 Daily 4pm–1am (3am Sat-Sun)
A rather kitsch decor, tasty Egyptian specialties and belly dancing. The non-gourmets come to smoke water pipes under the wise eye of Nefertiti. As a starter, do try the mezze (22 €); couscous 10 €.

**Trattoria
à Muntagnola (F** F4)
→ *Fuggerstr. 27*
Tel. 211 66 42
Daily 5pm–midnight
The Muntagnola ('small mountain') is a perfect name for this place. With grandma's crockery, images of the Madonna and the patron's funny jokes, this Italian trattoria does have a rustic charm. It has links with a group of children with AIDS, who are

MODO

STILWERK

KU'DAMM

invited once a week to have a tasty bowl of pasta. Dishes 10–21 €.

CAFÉS, BARS, TEAROOMS

Kleine Orangerie (F A1**)**
→ *Schloss Charlottenburg*
Tel. 322 20 21 Daily
9am–8pm (6pm winter)
Opposite the museums, at the far end of the castle's orangery, are an exotic glasshouse and a classic *Kneipe* for a coffee break, a *Flamkuchen* or a *Frühstücksbüfett* (served Sun 10am–2pm).

Luisen-Bräu (F A1**)**
→ *Luisenplatz 1*
Tel 341 93 88 Daily
9am–1am (2am Fri-Sat)
Two impressive copper vats tower above the wooden benches. They are used to brew three superb draft beers: Weizen (white with hints of fruit and fermenting agents), Hell (strong, wheaty, light beer) and Dunckel (full-flavored brown beer). All three are young and still cloudy.

Zwiebelfisch (F D3**)**
→ *Savignyplatz. 7-8*
Tel. 312 73 63
Daily noon–6am
A cult *Kneipe* since May, 1968, with an old clientele recalling their exploits while reading the newspapers, often arguing about politics in the smoky atmosphere.

Wirtshaus Wubke (F C3**)**
→ *Schlüterstr. 21*
Tel 31 50 92 17
Daily 11am–3am
A local *Kneipe* frequented by students, artists and regulars who will gladly strike up a conversation at the bar over a schnapps '43' or a draft beer.

OPERA

Deutsche Oper (F C2**)**
→ *Bismarckstr. 35*
Tel. 343 84 01
Ticket office: Mon-Sat
11am–one hour before the show; Sun 10am–2pm
West Berlin's opera house: lavish productions and international stars.

BARS, CLUBS

Die kleine Weltlaterne (F B4**)**
→ *Nestorstr. 22*
Tel. 89 09 36 16
Mon-Sat 8pm–3am
A Berlin myth since 1961! This late bar has acquired a reputation for spotting young talent, including painters and musicians. Even if it doesn't have the crowds of its heyday, the customers are loyal and a good ambience is assured. Jazz concerts on Thu and Sat.

A-Trane (F C3**)**
→ *Pestalozzistr. 105*
Tel. 313 25 50
Daily 9pm–2am (4am Fri-Sat). Concerts: daily 10pm
Small concert hall for a big club that bills the top jazz performers, but is keen to promote local talent.

Quasimodo (F D3**)**
→ *Kantstr. 12a*
Tel. 312 80 86
Daily 9pm. Concerts: 10pm (advance ticket sales from 5pm) www.quasimodo.de
Under the café is the jazz club, which not only puts on stars but also holds legendary jam sessions: jazz, soul, disco, blues. The audience is young(ish) and the mood is charged.

SHOPPING

Stilwerk (F C3**)**
→ *Kantstr. 17*
Tel. 31 51 50 Mon-Sat 10am–8pm (6pm Sat)
A commercial design center on five floors, all dedicated to homeware: big brands, but also local designers, antiquarians and even a piano supplier. Pretty interior garden.

Crines design (F D4**)**
→ *Bleibtreustr. 48*
Tel. 883 51 08 Mon-Sat 10am–8pm (6pm Sat)
A Berlin designer with a discreet, classic and elegant style, using linen in all its forms, and raw or weaved material that she makes into expansive tunics and large hats.

Ku'Damm (F D4**)**
→ *Kurfürstendamm*
The commercial hub of Charlottenburg: more than 2 miles of stores, art galleries, luxury hotels and theaters, which attract people of all ages.

New Steinbruch (F E4**)**
→ *Kurfürstendamm 237*
Tel. 88 55 21 26
Mon-Sat 11am–8pm (10am Sat)
Trendy, stylish fashions: satin pants, T-shirts and high boots for drag queens.

Ka De We (F F4**)**
→ *Tauentzienstr. 21-24*
Tel. 212 10
Mon-Fri 10am–8pm; Sat 9am–8pm
www.kadewe.de
This is Europe's largest department store (1907), with everything from haute couture to the complete range of Ritter Sport (chocolate bars in exotic flavors). The food hall on the top floor is a gourmet's paradise, with over a thousand types of ham and sausages, cheeses, breads and a buffet restaurant with panoramic views.

TIERGARTENUFER · LICHTENSTEIN.-

LANDWEHRKANAL

GÄSTEUFER

NEUER SEE

TIERGARTEN

STRASSE DES 17. JUNI

GROSSER WEG

TIERGARTENUFER

KLOPSTOCKSTR.

HANDELALLEE

HANSAPLATZ

BACHSTRASSE

ALTONAER STR.

AKADEMIE DER KÜNSTE

HANSA-VIERTEL

ST.-ANSGAR-KIRCHE

SCHLESWIGER UFER

SIEGMUNDS HOF

SPREE

HANSA-BRÜCKE

FLENSBURGER STR.

LESSINGSTR.

BUNDESRATUFER

ELBERFELDER STR

LINZEN-DORTSTR.

STRASSE

ESSENER STRASSE

STROM-STR.

LESSING-BRÜCKE

LEVETZOWSTRASSE

AGRICOLASTR.

TILE-WARDENBERG-STRASSE

WIKINGERUFER

WULLENWEBERSTR

HANSA-THEATER

ALT-MOABIT

GOTZKOWSKY-BRÜCKE

HELMHOLTZSTR.

HALLER-STR.

MORSE-STR.

PASCAL-STR.

DOVESTR.

DOVE-BRÜCKE

FRANKLINSTRASSE

EINSTEIN-UFER

SALZ-UFER

SALZ-UFER

TECHNISCHE UNIVERSITÄT BERLIN

MARCHSTRASSE

TICKETSTRASSE

EINSTEINSTRASSE

ENGLISCHE STRASSE

KÖNIGLICHE PORZELLANMANU-FAKTUR

ENGLISCHE BIBLIOTHEK

SENATS-BIBLIOTHEK

CHARLOTTENBURGER BRÜCKE

TECHNISCHE UNIVERSITÄT BERLIN

MÜLLER-BRESLAU-STRASSE

HERTZALLEE

FASANENSTRASSE

HOCHSCHULE DER KÜNSTE

KUNSTBIBLIOTHEK

HARDENBERGSTR.

HARDENBERGSTR.

FASANENSTR.

STEINPLATZ

SIESEBECKSTR.

THEATER-STR.

ERNST-REUTER-PLATZ

Ernst-Reuter-Platz

ERNST-REUTER-PL.

ALLEE

HARDENberg

Bröhan Museum
BRÖHAN MUSEUM

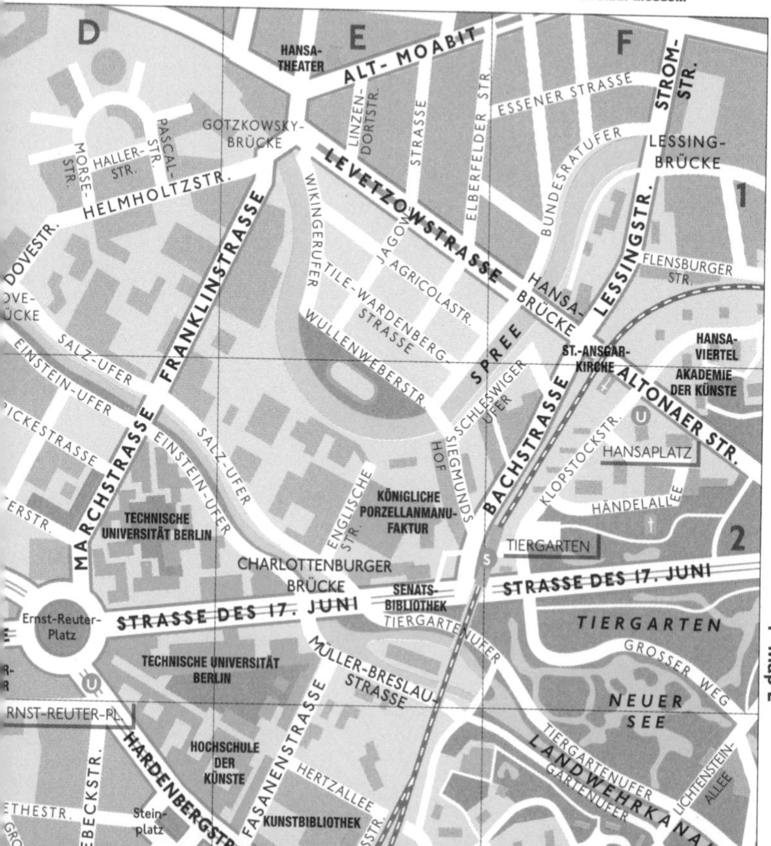

EGKOLLWITZ MUSEUM

SS CHARLOTTENBURG

MUSEUM FÜR VOR- UND FRÜHGESCHICHTE

SCHLOSSGARTEN

of 1971, include a
for the *Demoiselles*
non, cubist paintings
ortraits, etc.

yptisches
um (F A1)
loss-Str. 70
3 573 11
n 10am–6pm
te being 3,373 years
efertiti is still the most
iful woman in Berlin!
ust of Akhenaton's
s typical of the
ian works on display
Egyptian Museum:
ated curves and a
e style of
sentation that marked
ak with the cult of
. There is a large

department devoted to
Greco-Latin Egypt.

★ Schloss Charlottenburg (F A1)
→ Tel. (0331) 969 42 02
Tue-Fri 9am–5pm;
Sat-Sun 10am–5pm
Berlin's Baroque gem
(1695–1701), dedicated by
Frederick I (1688–1713) to
his wife Sophie Charlotte
and enlarged in 1740–6 by
Knobelsdorff for Frederick II.
Inside are the king's
sumptuous apartments, his
French painting collection
(including eight Watteaus),
the Chinese and Japanese
porcelain room and, in the
Galerie der Romantik,
masterpieces by Romantic

German painters such as
Caspar D. Friedrich.

★ Museum für Vor- und Frühgeschichte (F A1)
→ Schloss Charlottenburg
Tel. 32 67 48 11 Tue-Fri 10am–
6pm; Sat-Sun 11am–6pm
From the Paleolithic Period
to the Germanic Early
Middle Ages, the complete
pre- and protohistory of
Europe and the Near East.
Caucasian ceramics, a
ceremonial gold helmet
from the Bronze Age and
copies of the finest pieces
from the treasure of Troy
(jewelry and gold crockery)
discovered by Schliemann,
and seized by the Russians
in 1945.

★ Schlossgarten (F A1)
→ Tel. (0331) 969 42 02
Belvedere: April-Oct: Tue-Sun
10am–5pm. Nov-March: Tue-
Sun noon–4pm (5pm Sat-Sun)
Mausoleum: April-Oct:
Tue-Sun noon–5pm
Having strolled through the
Baroque garden by Siméon
Godeau (a pupil of André Le
Nôtre), you can explore the
paths and footbridges of the
landscaped garden (1819–
1928), designed by Lenné.
Don't miss the Neapolitan
pavilion by Schinkel, the
Belvedere by Carl Gotthard
Langhans and the
mausoleum of Queen Louise
(1776–1810), the mother of
Prussian nationalism.

FLYING TO BERLIN

From the US
Lufthansa
www.lufthansa.com
→ Tel. 800 645 3880
Delta Airlines
www.delta.com
→ Tel. 800 221 1212
Also check the following:
www.cheapflights.com
www.travelocity.com

From the UK
Lufthansa
www.lufthansa.co.uk
→ Tel. 0845 7737 747
AirBerlin
www.airberlin.de
→ Tel. 0870 738 8880
Ryanair *www.ryanair.com*
AirBerlin and Ryanair fly
from London Stansted to
Berlin Schönefeld.

TRAIN AT THE ZOOLOGISCHER GARTEN STATION

TAXI RANK ON SAVIGNYPLATZ

50–80 €

Pension Kreuzberg (D B3)
→ *Grossbeerenstr. 64,
Kreuzberg / Tel. 251 13 62*
A family-run pension in a
Gründerzeit building
(1870s). Fine period
staircase, spacious rooms,
attentive service and young
clientele. 52–65 €.

Pension Peters (F D3)
→ *Kantstr. 146,
Charlottenburg
Tel. 312 22 78*
This family-run hotel owned
by a sociable couple offers
15 bright, gaily colored
rooms. They also rent out
apartments in Mitte
(minimum three-day stay).
73–83 €. On the first floor
of the same building is
Hotel Pension Viola Nova
(Tel. 315 72 60) 75–85 €.

Hotel am Scheunenviertel (B B4)
→ *Oranienburgerstr. 38,
Mitte. Tel. 282 21 25*

A well-situated if rather
conventional hotel: perfect
for night revelers, right in
the heart of Mitte. If peace
and quiet is paramount, ask
for a room overlooking the
courtyard. 80 €.

Hotel Gunia (E B6)
→ *Eisenacherstr. 10,
Schöneberg. Tel. 218 59 40*
High ceilings, moldings
and gilt: this 300-year-old
building, listed as a historic
monument, has gorgeous
rooms that are full of charm
and character. 75–90 €.

Hotel-Pension Funk (F D4)
→ *Fasanenstr. 69,
Tel. 882 71 93*
A building once owned by
the silent movie star Asta
Nielsen, this hotel dates to
the end of 19th century,
with Jugendstil windows,
spacious rooms with over-
the-top decor. Ideally
located in a magnificent
tree-lined street near to the
Ku'Damm. 79–85 €.

80–110 €

Arco Hotel (E A6)
→ *Geisbergstr. 30,
Schöneberg. Tel. 235 14 80*
Small hotel in a peaceful
street. Comfortable rooms.
Breakfast in the garden
in summer. 82–92 €.

East-Side Hotel (C D4)
→ *Mühlenstr. 6,
Friedrichshain. Tel. 29 38 33*
www.eastsidecityhotel.de
Behind a listed façade,
this hotel-cum-art gallery
exhibits paintings in the
hall and dining room. There
are no paintings in the 36
modern rooms, but those
overlooking the street have
a view of the East Side
Gallery. 85 €.

Juncker's Hotel garni (C E3)
→ *Grünbergerstr. 21,
Friedrichshain Tel. 293 35 50*
Located in the center of
Friedrichshain. Rooms have
functional, slightly dated
furniture. 73–85 €.

TRAINS

Stations of arrival
→ *Tel. 01 805 99 66 33*
Zoologischer Garten
→ *Hardenbergplatz 11*
To the west (near the zoo).
Ostbahnhof
→ *Friedrichshain*
To the east (near East
Side Gallery).
Lehrter Bahnhof
The future central station
north of the Tiergarten
will open in 2006.

CARS

Wide, modern streets,
designed with cars in
mind. Avoid roadworks
(frequent) and rush hours
(7–9am, 4–6pm).

Driving
The Berliners always
abide by the highway
code: stop at orange
lights, give way to cyclists
and pedestrians on
crosswalks. At crossroads,
the first vehicle there has
right of way.

Speed limits
20 to 30 mph in the city.
No speed limit on
highways.

Parking
→ *1–3 €/hr, 20 €/day.*
It is difficult to park in the
center. Illegally parked
cars will be towed away.

TAXIS

Fares
→ *Pick up charge 2.50€,
then 0.10 €/km*

Short journey
→ *Fixed price 3 € (max.
2 kms/1¼ miles)*

Reservations
Würfelfunk *Tel. 210 101*
Taxi Funk *Tel. 443 322*
Funk Taxi *Tel. 261 026*
Cityfunk *Tel. 210 202*

AIRPORTS

Info tel. (0180) 500 01 86
Tegel
International routes (5 miles northwest of Berlin).
By bus
→ Bus 109, X9, TXL (2 €);
Duration: 30 mins
Stops: Zooligischer Garten, Unter den Linden and Alexanderplatz (TXL).
By taxi
→ 20 mins (15–20 €)
Tempelhof
Close to the city center. Domestic routes.
By subway
→ U6; 15 mins (2 €)
Schönefeld
The future central airport.
→ Train AirPortExpress; 30 mins (2 €)

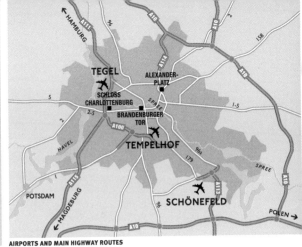

AIRPORTS AND MAIN HIGHWAY ROUTES

Unless otherwise stated, the prices given here are for a double room with bathroom and include breakfast. Reservations are essential six to eight weeks in advance from June to Sep, between Christmas and New Year's Eve, at Easter and when the city is hosting special events. Small pensions do not always accept credit cards.

PRIVATE ACCOMMODATION

Bed & Breakfast Berlin (B E3)
→ Mehringdamm 66, Kreuzberg Tel. 78 91 39 71
Mon–Fri 9am–6pm
This organization handles all apartment rentals and bed & breakfast options throughout the city (over 4,000 beds). Good facilities at modest prices and an excellent way of meeting Berliners. Rooms 27–54 €; apartments 54–98 €.

50 € and less

Youth hostels
Inexpensive dormitory accommodation, breakfast included. You must have an internation youth hostel card (available from the hostels).
Jugendgästehaus Berlin International
→ Kluckstr. 3, Tiergarten
Tel. 261 10 97
23.10 €; juniors 19 €.
Jugendherberge am Wannsee
→ Badeweg 1, Zehlendorf
Tel. 803 20 34
23.10 €; juniors 19 €.
Hotel Pegasus (C D3)
→ Str. der Pariser Kommune 35, Friedrichshain
Tel. 29 35 18 10
Between Karl-Marx Allee and East Side Gallery, this hotel offers non-smoking rooms with one to ten beds and one apartment for two people. Self-service kitchen (four people +), breakfast in

the garden. Dormitory 10 €/ person (double room 23 €/ person) + 2.50 € (sheets). Breakfast 2.70–3.50 €.
Globetrotter Hostel Odyssee (C E3)
→ Grünbergerstr. 23, Friedrichshain
Tel. 29 00 00 81
www.globetrotterhostel.de
Extravagantly decorated hotel that's run by former backpackers, 2 minutes from Simon-Dach-Str. In the bar-restaurant you can eat for 5 €. Dormitory 13–15 €/ person (double room 45 €); breakfast 3 €.
Circus, the Hostel (B D4)
→ Rosa-Luxemburg Str. 39-41, Mitte. Tel. 28 39 14 33
www.circus-berlin.de
Bright, clean rooms and impeccable service: very obliging staff, discounts for museums and shows, guided tours, informative documentation on Berlin, Internet access. Dormitory 15 €/person (double room

from 24 €/ person) + 2 € (sheets). Reserve a place well in advance. Buffet breakfast 3.50 €.
Mitte Backpackers Hostel (B A3)
→ Chausseestr. 102, Mitte
Tel. 28 39 09 65
www.backpacker.de
The oldest youth hostel in Mitte. Friendly atmosphere and multicolored frescos by former customers. Video room, self-service kitchen and, Internet access. It is also possible to rent bikes. Dormitory 16–18 €/ person (double room 24 €/ person) + 2.50 € (sheets). Breakfast for groups.
Hotel Transit (D A4)
→ Hagelbergerstr. 53, Kreuzberg
Tel. 789 04 70
In the heart of Kreuzberg, two floors of dormitories and rooms around the courtyard of a former Mietskaserne. Dormitory 19 € (double room 60 €).

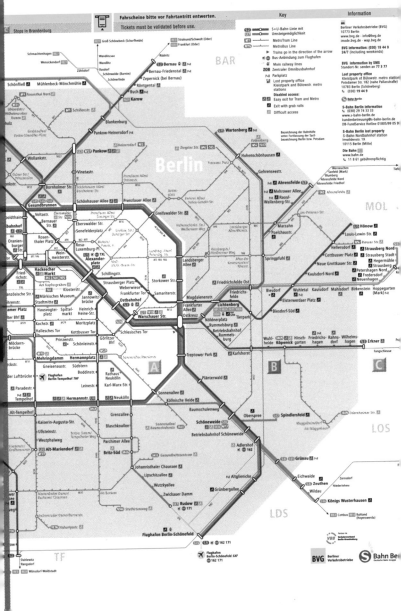

STREETCAR AT NIGHT

CYCLING IN FRONT OF THE REICHSTAG

tel Askanischer f (F C4)

→ *Kurführstendamm 53, arlottenburg*
881 80 33
w.askanischer-hof.de
ery elegant hotel with
ugendstil entrance hall,
autiful classic German
niture, thick carpet and
spacious rooms
rlooking the Ku'Damm.
peaceful and
torative stay. 117–130 €.

o € and over

k Inn Berlin (C A2)
Alexanderplatz, Mitte
23 89 43 33
*v.parkinn.com/berlinde_*
anderplatz
atch for Alexanderplatz,
gigantic hotel was
nally built to welcome
elers from neighboring
mmunist countries
ing the former East
many: 1,006 superbly
ipped rooms and

suites, and the most
stunning panorama of
Berlin since the picture
windows of this enormous
building were surmounted
by a casino. 170–210 €.

Hecker's Hotel (F D3)
→ *Grolmanstr. 35,*
Charlottenburg. Tel. 889 00
www.heckers-hotel.com
Centrally located, the
Hecker's is a modern
building with a very
appealing interior, with 69
stylishly furnished rooms
and excellent service.
Magnificent views from the
bay-windows of the fifth-
floor breakfast room. Roof
terrace in summer. 140–
200 €; breakfast 15 €.

LUXURY HOTELS

Hotel Adlon (A A3)
→ *Unter den Linden 77,*
Mitte. Tel. 226 111 11
www.hotel-adlon.de
Opposite the Brandenburg
Gate, this legendary palace,

inaugurated by William II,
used to welcome
Rockefeller, Charlie Chaplin
and Marlène Dietrich.
Rebuilt in 1997, it was
refurbished to a decadently
lavish standard.
300–350 €. Suites with a
view over Unter den Linden
or over Brandenburg Gate:
600–760 €.

Regent Schlosshotel
→ *Brahmsstr. 10,*
Wilmersdorf. Tel. 89 58 40
www.regenthotels.com
This palace, more a country
castle than a city hotel,
dates from the 1910s and,
with its marble and precious
wood fittings, is one of the
most luxurious hotels in
Berlin. Its amazing
refurbishment, in 1992, was
directed by Karl Lagerfeld
in return for a permanent,
magnificent suite. One
drawback: it is 30 minutes
away from the city center by
taxi (no buses or trams).
250 €; breakfast 22 €.

PUBLIC TRANSPORTATION

Information
→ *Tel. 194 49*
The BVG runs the three
areas of the network,
except the S-Bahn, which
is privately owned.
U-Bahn (subway)
Nine subway lines
covering the entire city.
S-Bahn (commuter train)
15 train lines operating a
service to the outskirts.
Bus
165 lines. Numerous
double-decker buses.
Streetcar
28 modernized lines,
mostly in East Berlin.
When?
→ *Daily 4am–2am*
Nachtlinien (night lines)
→ *Daily 2am–4am*
(every 30 mins)
Efficient night service:
56 bus lines, 5 tram lines
and 2 U-Bahn.
Nightlinesurfer
Brochure listing the
times of the Nachtlinien
from the center, and the
bars and clubs they pass.
Tickets
Ticket machines in
U-Bahn stations and
ticket offices in railroad
stations.
Kurzstrecke
→ *1.20 € for 6 stops*
(bus) or 3 subway stations
(U-Bahn/S-Bahn)
Einzelfahrausweis
→ *One-way ticket*
2.10 € for 2 hrs
Tageskarte
→ *6.10 € for 1 day*
7-Tage-Karte
→ *22 € for 1 week*
WelcomeCard
→ *19 € for 72 hrs*
Family ticket for 1 adult
with 3 children.

ILWAY STATIONS AND MAIN BUS ROUTES

CYCLES

Cycle lanes
On the sidewalk of most main roads.
U-Bahn and S-Bahn
It will cost you 2.10 € to take your bike with you, in the U-Bahn.
Rental
Fahrradstation
→ Hackesche Höfe
Tel. 28 38 48 48 / Mon-Fri 10am–7pm (4pm Sat)
Offices throughout Berlin (15 €/day, 50 €/week).
Call a Bike (Deutsche Bahn Rent)
→ Tel. 0700 05 22 5522
Rent a bike, with a phone call, at all major crossroads in the city. Maximum of 15€ / day.

tel Delta (E C5)
Pohlstr. 58, Tiergarten
. 26 00 20
is contemporary building ers rooms with designer niture, all different and ell equipped. 99–133 €.
**tel-Pension
astanien Hof (B** D3)
*Kastanien Allee 65,
enzlauer Berg. Tel. 44 30 50*
ell-located hotel, set tween Mitte and enzlauer Berg; it is also ry near the delightful onskirchplatz. Large, ight rooms. Bikes for nt. 103–113 €.
**tist Riverside
otel (A** C1)
*Friedrichstr. 106, Mitte
l. 284 900
ww.tolles-hotel.de*
ear Oranienburgerstrasse d Unter den Linden, this gendstil hotel has been ecorated to resemble a eater or movie theater. ome rooms offer splendid ews over the Spree.

Discounts for artists and musicians. Spa. 90–120 €; breakfast 9 €.
MitART Pension (B B4)
→ *Linienstr. 139-140, Mitte
Tel. 28 39 04 30*
The MitART has a new address but remains an excellent choice for your stay: it is quiet and within walking distance of the city center. The owner is passionate about the painters she chooses to exhibit everywhere in the hotel. The 30 rooms are spacious and well-decorated. 105 €.

110–130 €

**Hotel Kunstlerheim
Luise (B** A4)
→ *Luisenstr. 19, Mitte
Tel. 28 44 80
www.kuenstlerheim-luise.de*
Each of the 48 rooms in this hotel is a work in its own right, designed by an artist whose name it

adopts. For instance, there is the 'dream' by David Mammel: an immense dark wooden bed covering the entire floor, with a canvas on the wall by the painter. Bear in mind that some rooms are reserved several months in advance. 85–132 €.
Hotel Art Nouveau (F C4)
→ *Leibnizstr. 59, Charlottenburg
Tel. 327 74 40
www.hotelartnouveau.de*
The rooms are decorated in a variety of colors: red, yellow and blue, which are inspired by Italian or Japanese paintings. This is a place where charm and comfort are of utmost importance. 110–120 €.
**Hotel-Pension
Honigmond (B** B3)
→ *Tieckstrs. 12, corner of Borsigstr., Mitte
Tel. 284 45 50
www.honigmond-berlin.de*
Above a restaurant, this

pension is several minutes from Oranienburger Tor and has 20 bright, comfortable rooms. 120 €; breakfast 7.50 €.
**Dietrich-Bonhoeffer-
Haus (A** C1)
→ *Ziegelstr. 30, Mitte
Tel. 28 46 70
www.hotel-dbh.de*
Just behind the Tacheles, between alternative Berlin and historic Berlin, this Protestant hotel has its own chapel. Well-equipped, modern rooms. 120 €.
**Hotel Riehmers
Hofgarten (D** B3)
→ *Yorckstr. 83, Kreuzberg
Tel. 78 09 88 00
www.hotel-riehmers-hofgarten.de*
Large, bright, well-equipped rooms elegantly decorated by a contemporary designer. Excellent gastronomic restaurant on the first floor. 123–138 €.

Index of streets, monuments and places of interes

Streets